Catholic Spirituality
A Grace Driven Life

FR. JOHN J. PASQUINI, TH.D.

An Ecce Fides Publication

Instituti ratione, fides, et cultura

Cataloguing Information:
Philosophy, Religion; Theology

Text has been deemed free of doctrinal errors.

An Ecce Fides Publication

Instituti ratione, fides, et cultura

Purchases can be made through **amazon.com**

Printed in the United States of America

Table of Contents

Introduction

There are two realities we deal with every day of our lives. On the one hand we desire a life of happiness, peace and contentment, and on the other hand we recognize that life comes with suffering. How do we reconcile these two realities?

As Christians we believe that Christ reconciles these two realities; that in Christ, the Reconciler, we can have a taste of happiness, a taste of peace and contentment, even amidst a life that inevitably and unavoidably comes with suffering, with trials and tribulations.

Holiness is a voyage toward light, happiness and peace. It is a journey toward "wholeness" and toward authentic "humanness." In a world that thirsts and aches for meaning and purpose, the spiritual life provides the means for attaining this purpose and meaning.

Catholic Spirituality summarizes and explains the best of Catholic prayer and spiritual development. It is a blueprint whereby day-to-day Catholics can find fulfillment.

I
The Awakening

People are hungry for God. People are hungry for love. Are you aware of that? Do you know that? Do you see that? Do you have eyes to see? Quite often we look but we don't see. We are all passing through this world. We need to open our eyes and see.[1]

Mother Teresa

When one's eyes are open to the reality of God, then one can be said to be awakened. There is a point in life where one is faced with the reality that there is something which is beyond the self and the here and now, something which transcends the limits of one's being. This moment is a moment of choice. Does one seek to explore and enter into this mystery of that which is not limited to the self or does one repress the experience? The choice made is the choice that will help govern one's life.

What attracts you to God?

One is awakened and moved to follow the ways of grace by being enlightened to the presence of God. Traditionally, people have been attracted to God in the following ways:

Meaning and Purpose

People are often awakened or attracted to God because God gives them a sense of meaning and purpose in life (cf. Dt. 6:24-25). One recognizes that one must be more than some complex organism that is born, lives, struggles, and dies in emptiness. Life in many ways would be a farce if that were so. Life would be inevitably on the edge of disintegration. There must be more to life than mere existence, than mere survival.

Life needs purpose and meaning, a purpose and meaning that transcends the here and now.

God provides this purpose and meaning, for he is the source and summit of all meaning and purpose.

Truth

Many are attracted to God because he is Truth (1 Jn. 4:6). Such people seek truth in life, no matter where they may find it. Such people find great comfort in God because he is the goal of their quest, truth itself. Hence, life

---

[1] *Mother Teresa*, *One Heart Full of Love* (Ann Arbor: Servant Publications, 1984), 11.

becomes for such individuals a delving into the mysteries of God, which consumes the entirety of their lives and gives them their ultimate joy.

Good

Some people find God by seeing the good around them. Malcolm Muggeridge, a world-renowned reporter for the BBC, was such a person in many respects. It was in seeing the good that was in the heart of Mother Teresa of Calcutta that he was able to find Christ. In Mother Teresa he saw Jesus Christ, and his life would never be the same again. God is good, and those who have found authentic goodness have found God (cf. Rm. 12:2).

Beautiful

Many are attracted to God because they see in the beauty of creation the handprint of God. For them all of creation echoes the beauty and providence of God. To find authentic beauty is to find the source of all beauty, God (cf. Wis. 13:3).

The Four Ways

While it is true that most people will find an affinity for one of the above ways in which we are attracted to God, all the above ways should be a part of one's attraction to God.

The spiritual journey is a chase after the heart of God, and this entails continual growth and maturity into the ways of God.

A Hardened Heart

> I felt at the time that religion would impede my work. I wanted to have nothing to do with the religion of those I saw all around me. I felt that I must turn from it as from a drug. I felt it indeed to be an opiate of the people and not a very attractive one, so I hardened my heart. It was a conscious and deliberate process.[2]
>
> *Dorothy Day*

Dorothy Day would eventually respond to God and soften her heart and become a world leader in the Church's work for the poor and the disenfranchised.

A hardened heart is one of the most problematic dilemmas that one can experience along one's journey in life (cf. Jn. 12:40). It is so problematic

---

[2] Dorothy Day, *The Long Loneliness* (New York: Curtis Books, 1972), 10.

because it is so difficult to overcome and to heal. There is perhaps nothing more obtrusive to the gift of grace than a heart that is unwilling to open itself up to the possibility of an all-engulfing God.

A hardened heart is a frightened heart, a heart unwilling to take a chance at experiencing anything beyond its comfort level. There is a fear that what one may find if one opens one's heart will be too overwhelming to deal with.

A hardened heart is most often the consequence of some unresolved issue or deep psychological scar that has never been dealt with properly. One cannot conquer what one does not recognize.

When one examines the lives of atheists, it is astonishingly common to find these people lacking in good fatherly figures. It is difficult to pray "Our Father who art in heaven" when the only experience of a father has been one that has been experienced as evil, mean-spirited, or non-existent. When looking at the lives of the world's major atheists, such as men like Nietzsche, one is struck by this lack of fatherly guidance. For people such as this, often a miracle is necessary to soften the heart.

It is here where the communion of saints becomes so significant (cf. Jn. 2:1-14; Rev. 5:8). The communion of the faithful here on earth and in heaven has a profound effect on the softening of hearts throughout the world, for by themselves people with hardened hearts are much too weak to respond to the grace that is being showered upon them. A tragic event or the power of the prayers of the saints is often the only way these people soften their hearts. In many ways, they are very much like addicts. They often need to hit rock bottom before they can acknowledge the need of another. It is through the prayers of others, known and unknown, that the world's hearts are softened.

One must, thus, never underestimate the power of praying for others. St. Monica prayed for thirty years for the conversion of her son, Augustine. Her prayers were successful in softening his heart and he became the great St. Augustine.

II
Foundational Points

The Dignity of the Human Person

Christ ...in the very revelation of the mystery of the Father and of his love, makes man fully manifest to himself and brings to light his exalted vocation.[3]

The human person has been created in the "image and likeness of God" (cf. Gen. 1:27). This image and likeness to God is seen in a person's expression of his or her powers of the intellect, will, and freedom.[4] However, it is in Christ, the Savior and Redeemer, that the divine image is ennobled and most perfectly manifested.[5]

The human person is gifted with an immortal and spiritual nature. The human person is the only act of creation that God willed for its own unique sake.[6] From the very moment of conception, the human person is born to eternal life.[7]

The human person has been endowed with the gift of freely seeking, perceiving and loving the good and the true. This is a gift that is found at the very core of the person. It is a natural law that has been embedded into the core of a person's conscience.[8]

At the beginning of time humanity had a choice to live with God or live without him (cf. Gen. 3:1-24). The choice to live without God caused a wound, a wound that would forever affect human nature. This wound would come to be known as original sin, a sin of such a great nature that it destroyed the possibility of eternal life and happiness.

God would not allow humanity to remain separated from eternal life with him. He sent his only begotten Son to restore us to new life in God (2 Cor. 5:17). Sin was forgiven by the merits of Christ.

Yet even though the deep, penetrating cut of original sin was cleansed by the blood of Christ on the cross, a scar persisted, a scar called concupiscence. Thus, scarred, but not destroyed, human nature is forever tempted and inclined, on this earthly journey, toward evil and error.

---

[3] GS 22.
[4] Ibid., 17.
[5] Ibid., 22.
[6] Ibid., 24.
[7] CCC 1703.
[8] GS 15-17; CCC 1704-1707.

Thus, human nature is involved in a spiritual battle, a battle between good and evil, light and darkness (cf. Jn. 1:5; 8:12; 12:35).[9] It is a spiritual battle, however, that is fought with the gift of God's grace that was restored to us in Christ Jesus.

The gift of grace is that gift that enables one to become a child of God (cf. 1 Jn. 5:1). A person, through the merits of Christ and the gift of grace, is able to grow in the spiritual and moral life.[10]

Grace[11]

> Grace is...rooted in us, and worked into us like leaven, from our earliest years, until the thing thus present becomes fixed in a man like a natural endowment, as if it were one substance with him. But, for the man's own good, it manages him in many different ways, after its own pleasure. Sometimes the fire flames out and kindles more vehemently; at other times more gently and mildly. The light that it gives kindles up at times and shines with unusual brightness; at others it abates and burns low. The lamp is always burning and shining, but when it is specially trimmed, it kindles up with intoxication with the love of God....[12]
>
> *Pseudo-Marcarius*

The Christian is one who responds to live life in love, the love of God, neighbor, and self (cf. Lk. 10:27). The Christian is one who is moving toward total authenticity, toward total and full *human-ness*. The Christian is radically oriented to respond to one's ultimate destiny of union with the self-communicating God of love. The spiritual journey is a call to be awakened, purified, and illuminated to one's true nature. The spiritual life is a call to reality, to see reality as it truly is and to see one's own self as one truly is.

Grace is the fundamental reality of the spiritual journey. Grace is a participation in the life of God, which justifies, sanctifies, deifies, and makes one a co-heir with God (cf. Jn. 1:12-18; 17:3; Rom. 8:14-17; 2 Cor. 5:17-18; 2 Pet. 1:3-4). Grace is the gift of God himself—the giver is the gift.[13] Grace is a

---

[9] GS 13; CCC 1706.

[10] CCC 1709.

[11] Cf. CCC 1996-2005. See Henri de Lubac, *A Brief Catechesis on Nature and Grace*, trans. Brother Richard Arnandez (San Francisco: Ignatius Press, 1984) for a historical survey of the relationship between nature and grace.

[12] *Fifty Spiritual Homilies of St. Macarius the Great*, trans. A.J. Mason (Willits: Eastern Orthodox Books, 1974), Homily VIII, n. 2.

[13] Karl Rahner, *Foundations of the Christian Faith: An Introduction to the Idea of Christianity*, trans.

supernatural, gratuitous, and perfecting gift and favor that is always present—existentially present—at the very core of the person waiting to be accepted or rejected in freedom.[14] When a person truly seeks to understand his or her very core, he or she is bound to end up finding grace, finding God.

Habitual Grace

Habitual grace or sanctifying grace is that gift of the Holy Spirit that gives an individual the capacity to act in accordance with the demands of faith, hope and love. It is with the person, unless eliminated by mortal sin.[15]

Actual Graces

Flares of grace, divine touches, wounds of love, darts of love are often what are referred to as actual graces.[16] An actual grace is a gift, a special flare or moment of God's self-communicating, that enables a person to act in a salutary, beneficial, curative, and holy manner. Often this flare of grace is experienced as an interior impulse, attraction, inspiration, illumination, or interior light. At times it is experienced as a special moment of strength, courage or endurance. At other times it arouses good thoughts and feelings that seem to come from nowhere.[17]

> The life of grace is a taste of heaven, for it is a taste of God.[18]
>
> St. Thomas Aquinas

Grace and Nature[19]

We are body and soul (cf. 1 Thess. 5:13; Mt. 10:28). This reality has a profound impact on the spiritual life. If a person's body is healthy, psychologically and physically, grace has a much more profound impact on the spiritual life of the person, depending on the person's free-will response to God's self-communication. If, however, the body is ill, psychologically or physically, then the spiritual life is subject to difficulties in its progress.

---

by William V. Dych (New York: Crossroad Publishing, Co., 1984), 120.

[14] Cf. Rahner, *Foundations*, 128.

[15] Cf. Ia, q. 105, a.4; Ia IIae, q. 9, a.6; q. 10, a.4; q. 109, a.2, 3, 4, 10. All quotations and citations regarding St. Thomas Aquinas' *Summa* will always be cited in full in this text in order to alleviate confusion.

[16] Cf. *Spiritual Canticle*, st. 1, nos. 17-22; *Living Flame*, St. 1, no. 27. All quotations and citations from St. John of the Cross and St. Teresa of Avila are taken from the Institute of Carmelite Studies' editions.

[17] Cf. Ia, q. 105, a.4; Ia IIae, q. 9, a.6, q. 10, a.4; q. 109, a.2, 3, 4, 10.

[18] Cf. IIa IIae, q. 24, a.3 ad 2um; Ia IIae, q. 69, a.2.

[19] See De Lubac, *Nature and Grace*.

Likewise, if the person's spiritual life is weak, then a person's soul will be unhealthy, and so too will the body. The body will be subject to all kinds of psychological and related physical ailments. Hence, one is called to foster a healthy physical and spiritual life. If one's bodily existence is ailing, one should seek all the medical attention within one's capacity (i.e., medication, counseling, etc.) (cf. 1 Tim. 5:23). If one's spiritual life is unhealthy, one must seek a deeper conversion so as to promote a healthy bodily existence.

What about the cross? It is true that at times, despite all the medical attention one may have access to, the body bears incurable wounds. This is the mystery of the cross and the mystery of grace. Despite it all, Christ, the *Great Physician*, takes the weaknesses and wounds of a person and elevates them into strengths: Who better to understand a person's weakness than one who is weak?

Grace not only builds upon nature, but it also heals and elevates it to new heights (cf. 2 Cor. 12:10). Thus, grace is often the source of the healing of many ailments, whether physical, psychological, or spiritual.

Grace and Merit

[Faith] apart from works is dead (cf. Jms. 2:14-26).

Grace and good works are inseparable realities in the life of a person. Authentic faith always points to authentic holy works and authentically holy works are always marked by authentic faith. It is this reality between grace and merit that exemplifies the reality of the spiritual journey, since all are called to perfection (cf. Rom. 8:28-30) and the spiritual battle (cf. 2 Tim. 4).

Justification[20]

Justification flows from grace. Grace provides the person with the possibility of entering into the Paschal Mystery--Jesus' life, death, resurrection and ascension. Consequently, grace justifies a person. It makes one a "new creation" in God (cf. Rom. 3:22; 6:3-4, 8-11; 1 Cor. 12; Jn. 15:1-4).

There are essentially six key aspects in regard to justification:

1) "Justification is not only the remission of sins, but also the sanctification and renewal of the interior man," conversion (cf. Mt. 4:17).[21]

---

[20] Cf. CCC 1987-1995.
[21] Council of Trent (1547): DS 1528.

14

2) Justification detaches a person from sin, from enslavement, through the continual offer of forgiveness. It reconciles and heals the person's innermost being.

3) Justification is the acceptance of God's righteousness. It is the acceptance of the life of faith, hope, and love—a life in obedience to God's will.

4) Justification has been merited by Christ's Passion (cf. Rom. 3:21-26). Justification implies a blood atonement for sins and the gift of eternal life through the gift of baptism into Christ's life, death, and resurrection (either by a baptism of desire, blood, or water).

5) Justification establishes the cooperation between grace and freedom. On God's part there is the continual offer of grace. On the person's part there is the demand for continual conversion (cf. Mt. 4:17) and the continual assent to faith. It demands response to the Spirit and cooperation in divine love.

6) Justification entails the sanctification of the whole being (cf. Rom. 6:19, 22).

The Moral Law[22]

The moral law is that which guides a person on the spiritual journey. There are three kinds of moral laws, all of which are interrelated, and all of which find their source of being at the core of the person (cf. Phil. 2:12-13).

Natural Law

Natural law finds its impetus in God's wisdom and the immutable gift of reason.[23] The goal of the moral law is life in Christ (cf. Rom. 10:4).

> The natural law is written and engraved in the soul of each and every man, because it is human reason ordaining him to do good and forbidding him to sin.... But this command of human reason would not have the force of law if it were not the voice and interpreter of a higher reason to which our spirit and our freedom must be submitted.[24]
>
> Where then are these rules written, if not in the book of that light we call the truth? In it is written every just law; from it the law passes into the heart of the man who does justice, not that it

---

[22] Cf. CCC 1950-1974; 2031-2046.
[23] Cf. GS 10.
[24] Leo XIII, *Li bertas praestantissimum*, 597, quoted in CCC 1954.

migrates into it, but that it places its imprint on it, like a seal on a ring that passes unto wax, without leaving the ring.[25]

Leo XIII/ St. Augustine

The natural law is nothing other than the light of understanding in us by God; through it we know what we must do and what we must avoid. God has given this light or law at creation.[26]

St. Thomas Aquinas

Through the natural law one practices that which is good and attends to one's eternal destiny, one's salvation.[27] The natural law promotes the dignity and the rights and duties of the person.

Revealed Law

Divine revelation, which is found in the Sacred Scriptures and Sacred Tradition, reveals that which is in the heart.[28] It aids, enlightens, and clarifies the natural moral law, which sin can often cloud.[29] The moral law finds its fulfillment in the law of love.

Ecclesiastical Law

The laws or precepts of the Church nourish and strengthen a person's ability to perceive and follow the innate natural law. The emphasis on these laws is on attending Mass on a regular basis, receiving communion, seeking reconciliation, fasting and abstaining from meat on appointed days, joining in the missionary efforts of the Church, and so on.

The Moral Virtues

To live well is nothing other than to love God with all one's heart, with all one's soul and with all one's efforts; from this it comes about that love is kept whole and uncorrupted (through temperance). No misfortune can disturb it (and this is fortitude). It obeys only [God] (and this is justice), and is careful in discerning things, so as not to be surprised by deceit or trickery (and this is prudence).[30]

---

[25] St. Augustine, *De Trin.* 14, 15, 21: PL 42, 1052.
[26] St. Thomas Aquinas, *Dec. praec.* I.
[27] Cf. GS 89.
[28] St. Augustine, *En. In Ps.* 57, 1: PL 36, 673.
[29] Pius XII, *Humani generis*: DS 3876; cf. *Dei Filius* 2: DS 3005.
[30] St. Augustine, *De moribus eccl.* 1, 25, 46: PL 32, 1330-1331.

A holy person is a virtuous person (cf. Wis. 8:7; Phil. 4:8). A holy person is a virtuous person who seeks "to be like God"[31]; that is, to be in the image and likeness to which he or she was originally created in (cf. Gen. 1:27). Therefore, in order for one to comprehend the path that grace draws one toward, one needs to comprehend the virtues. There are two types of virtues, the acquired moral virtues and the infused moral virtues.

Acquired Moral Virtues

The acquired moral virtues are acquired by the repetition of acts under the direction of the light of *natural right reason*. Grace is not required to acquire these natural virtues.

For example, by the natural light of human reason and discipline one can learn to be just, temperate, courageous, and prudent.

Infused Moral Virtues

Infused moral virtues require a person's response to grace. Through a person's response to grace, the acquired virtues, which are guided by right reason, are elevated to a level that surpasses the limits of right reason alone. Only God can empower a person with infused moral virtues, for they are by nature supernatural acts of grace. These virtues are directed toward a person's supernatural last end and consequently are essential for eternal life.[32]

The Relationship Between Acquired and Infused Moral Virtues

Holiness at whatever level requires the proper interaction of the acquired and infused moral virtues.[33] The proper interaction of the acquired moral virtues and the infused moral virtues make for the perfect spiritual person. In such a case, all of a person's life, in all its aspects, is in perfect harmony, like five fingers on a hand.[34]

The Theological Virtues (cf. 1 Cor. 13:13)

---

[31] St. Gregory of Nyssa, *De beatitudinibus*, 1: PG 44, 1200D.
[32] Cf. Ia IIae, q. 63, a.3, 4; q. 109, a.3.
[33] Cf. IIa IIae, q. 24, a.9.
[34] Cf. Ia IIae, q. 66, a.2.

The theological virtues of faith, hope, and love empty a person of all that is not for the honor and glory of God and fills such a person with God's self-communicating, cleansing presence. A person is empty to be filled.

The human virtues are grounded in the theological virtues (cf. 2 Pet. 1:4), which enable a person to be animated, informed, and enlivened in Christ. Faith frees the intellect to soar into realms of knowing it had never before experienced (Is. 55:8-9). It penetrates the deep mysteries of God that are beyond the natural and rational boundaries.[35] Hope empties the memory of the unhealthy, worldly passing allurements that seek to compete with the bliss that comes from God. Love unburdens the will and the heart of all that is false and fleeting and helps one to cling to that which is of God.[36] In faith, hope, and love one moves toward union with God, toward peace, happiness, and light.[37]

Gifts of the Spirit

The gifts of the Holy Spirit are essential to the spiritual growth of the person and are essential for salvation.[38] The gifts of the Spirit are what transform a hardened heart into a docile heart, a heart ready for God's engulfing presence.[39]

Knowledge, understanding, wisdom, counsel, piety, fortitude, and fear of the Lord are the traditional gifts of the Spirit (Is. 11:2f). The gift of knowledge helps one to understand God's creation; the gift of understanding helps one to delve into the sphere of truth; the gift of wisdom, the highest of the gifts, aids one to perceive the divine; the gift of counsel helps one to direct one's actions according to God's will; the gift of piety aids one in proper worship; the gift of fortitude, helps one fight off the fears that confront one in the works of God, and the gift of fear of the Lord protects one from falling into disorderly temptations.

The Evangelical Counsels

The evangelical counsels are poverty, chastity, and obedience. They lead to spiritual perfection and the healing of moral wounds. *Poverty* is empowered by the theological virtue of hope, *chastity* by the theological virtue of love, and *obedience* by the theological virtue of faith. The counsels, thus, render to God what is due to him.[40]

---

[35] Cf. *Ascent*, BK II, Ch. 1, no. 1.
[36] Cf. Ibid., BK II, Ch. 6, nos. 1-4.
[37] Cf. Ibid., BK II, Ch. 4, nos. 2-3.
[38] Cf. Ia IIae, q. 68, a.2.
[39] Cf. Ia IIae, q. 68, a.3.
[40] Cf. Ia IIae, q. 108, a.4; IIa IIae, q. 186, a.3, 4, 5, 7.

The evangelical counsels take on a special meaning for those in religious life and holy orders. They, in a unique manner, point to life in heaven. *Poverty* points to the reality that in heaven we will have no need, *celibacy* points to the fact that in heaven there will be no marrying, and *obedience* points to the fact that our eternal destiny will be consumed with being in perfect harmony with our Creator.

The Beatitudes (Mt. 5:3-12)

Blessed are the poor in spirit,
for theirs is the kingdom of heaven.
Blessed are they who mourn,
for they will be comforted.
Blessed are the meek,
for they will inherit the land.
Blessed are they who hunger and thirst for righteousness,
for they will be satisfied.
Blessed are the merciful,
for they will be shown mercy.
Blessed are the clean of heart,
for they will see God.
Blessed are the peacemakers,
for they will be called children of God.
Blessed are they who are persecuted for the sake of righteousness,
for theirs is the kingdom of heaven.

Blessed are you when they insult you and persecute you and utter every kind of evil against you [falsely] because of me. Rejoice and be glad, for your reward will be great in heaven. Thus they persecuted the prophets who were before you.[41]

The beatitudes flow from the gifts of the Spirit and dispose a person to obey these gifts.[42] The beatitude of being "poor in spirit" promotes confidence in God and complete dependence on God (cf. Is. 61:1; Zep. 2:3). It also engenders a humble predisposition. The beatitude of being "mournful" is that beatitude which fosters recognition of God's consolation and comfort. The beatitude of being "meek," engenders the recognition of one's place in the kingdom of God (cf. Ps. 37:11). The beatitude of "hungering and thirsting for righteousness" promotes conformity to God's will and a willing submission to God's plan of salvation for all. The beatitude of being "merciful" properly orders the virtue of justice in accordance to the "spirit" of the law as opposed

---

[41] NABRE
[42] Cf. Ia IIae, q. 70, a.2.

19

to the "letter of the law." The beatitude of being "pure of heart" is that assurance that God's presence will always be with the pure of heart (cf. Ps. 24:4; 42:3). The beatitude of being a "peacemaker" is one that promotes peace in one's heart and in the hearts of others. It promotes a docile, gentle spirit that is ordered to the providential plan of God. The beatitude that entails being unjustly "persecuted" is that beatitude which empowers one to seek justice at whatever cost, even at the cost to one's life. To live the life of the beatitudes is to live the life that brings one to experience the ultimate in happiness in a world filled with trials and tribulations.

The beatitudes express the human person's vocation as a spiritual being. They shed light on a Christian's duties and attitudes. They sustain hope amidst a world of trials and tribulations.[43] They "proclaim the blessings and rewards already secured, however dimly, for Christ's disciples."[44]

The beatitudes express a person's innermost desire, that person's desire for happiness. This desire for happiness has been placed at the very core of the human person in order to draw him or her to God, the source of all happiness.[45]

> We all want to live happily; in the whole human race there is no one who does not assent to this proposition, even before it is fully articulated.[46]

> How is it, then, I seek you, Lord? Since in seeking you, my God, I seek a happy life, let me seek you so that my soul may live, for my body draws life from my soul and my soul draws life from you.[47]

> God alone satisfies.[48]
>
> *St. Augustine/ St. Thomas Aquinas*

St. Thomas Aquinas says that another word for God is "happiness." The sad reality of life is that many people today, as in all generations, have failed to recognize that God alone is happiness and that God alone satisfies. Such people, sadly, end up chasing after things that appear at first sight to bring about happiness but in the end only bring about disappointment. Some people seek to fill this innate desire for happiness with fame, power, human

---

[43] CCC 1717.
[44] Ibid.
[45] Ibid., 1718.
[46] St. Augustine, *De moribus eccl.* 1, 3, 4: PL 32, 1312.
[47] Ibid., *Confessions*, 10, 20: PL 32, 791.
[48] St. Thomas Aquinas, *Expos. In symb. Apost.* I.

achievement, drugs, illicit sex, and so forth, yet they never find peace and contentment.

> All bow down before wealth. Wealth is that to which the multitude of men pay an instinctive homage. They measure happiness by wealth; and by wealth they measure respectability.... It is a homage resulting from a profound faith...that with wealth he may do all things. Wealth is one idol of the day and notoriety is a second.... Notoriety, or the making of a noise in the world—it may be called "newspaper fame"—has come to be considered a great good in itself, and a ground of veneration.[49]
>
> *John Henry Newman*

If only people could recognize what the great saints have always recognized: That our soul will only rest in God (cf. Ps. 62:1).

The beatitudes challenge and confront people. They force people to make choices regarding their eternal destiny.

Freedom, Responsibility, and Personal Becoming

> Man is rational and therefore like God; he is created with free will and is master over his acts.[50]

At the core of a person's nature or essence, intrinsic to him or her, is that person's freedom. Freedom is the means by which a person primarily becomes something. A person is so free that he or she has within his or her being the capacity to take control of his or her basic nature. A person is able to determine what he or she is and what he or she is to be. Therefore, at the heart of the definition of the person is the reality that the person is one who is open to becoming.[51]

Freedom is an openness to that which is beyond—a movement toward fulfillment. Because freedom is open and a movement toward fulfillment it allows for self-causation, that is, the power to become. Freedom entails a possibility for self-achievement, self-becoming. In freedom we can realize our potential. In the words of Karl Rahner,

---

[49] John Henry Newman, "Saintliness the Standard of Christian Principle," in *Discourses to Mixed Congregations* (London: Longmans, Green and Co., 1906), V, 89-90.
[50] St. Irenaeus, *Adv. Haeres.* 4, 4, 3: PG 7/1, 983.
[51] Cf. Karl Rahner, *Hearers of the Word*, trans. Michael Richards (New York: Herder and Herder, 1969), 3-179.

...[Freedom] is a permanent constituent of man's nature. The true nature of freedom appears precisely in this, that in the Christian revelation it is the cause of both absolute salvation and absolute rejection by the final judgment of God.... In the Christian view...man is, through his freedom, capable of determining.... Through his free decision he is rather truly good or evil in the very ground of his being, and thus, in the Christian view, his final salvation or loss is already present, even though perhaps still hidden.[52]

The person endowed with grace is on a journey—whether he is aware of it or not—toward the perfection of Christ, the God-man, the fully divine, fully human being. By seeking the God that dwells within, one can find one's true human potential, and by seeking to find one's full humanity, one can find the divine within whether in an explicit way or an implicit way.[53]

Christians are called into the *Mystery of God*. By making the choice to enter into this mystery one is making a choice to enter into the spiritual life, the beginning of the mystical life.[54]

The Limitations of Human Freedom

Human freedom is not absolute. It is limited and subject to errors. It is limited in that it demands obedience to the natural law that resides at the core of every person, and it is subject to error in that it is subject to the slavery and blindness that is associated with sin. As the *Catechism* states, "By deviating from the moral law man violates his own freedom, becomes imprisoned within himself, disrupts neighborly fellowship, and rebels against divine truth."[55] Human history attests to the sad consequences that result from the sinful abuse of freedom.

The Christian is called to live a life in imitation of Christ. The Savior who saved us from the slavery of sin is the one that all are called to imitate, for in this imitation is found the ultimate in liberation and freedom (cf. Gal. 5:1; Jn. 8:32; 2 Cor. 17; Rom. 8:21). In the grace of Christ one is educated and nourished in the ways of authentic freedom.[56]

---

[52] Karl Rahner, *Grace in Freedom*, trans. Hilda Graef (New York: Herder and Herder, 1969), 210-211.
[53] Cf. Rahner, *Foundations*, 1-459.
[54] Cf. Karl Rahner, *Theology of Renewal*, trans. Cecily Hastings (New York: Sheed and Ward, 1964), 73.
[55] CCC 1740
[56] Ibid., 1741-1742.

In the early stages of the spiritual journey, the imitation of Christ is quite difficult, and therefore one's sense of freedom and liberation is curtailed.

Moral Conscience

Deep within his conscience man discovers a law which he has not laid upon himself but which he must obey. Its voice, ever calling him to love and to do what is good and to avoid evil, sounds in his heart at the right moment.... For man has in his heart a law inscribed by God.... His conscience is man's most secret core and his sanctuary. There he is alone with God whose voice echoes in his depths.[57]

Gadium et Spes

A person entrusted with this innate moral law, this conscience, is obliged to be faithful to this moral law in choosing what is right and just. In so doing one recognizes the ultimate in truth, truth itself, God himself, Christ himself.

Conscience is a messenger of him, who, both in nature and in grace, speaks to us behind a veil, and teaches and rules us by his representatives. Conscience is the aboriginal Vicar of Christ.[58]

John Henry Newman

Conscience directs a person to conversion and to hope. It enables one to recognize the evil one has done and to consequently ask for God's forgiveness. Conscience also helps one recognize the good and the power of hope. It directs one away from evil, unhappiness, despair, and moves one toward happiness, peace, and light.

The Formation of Conscience

One has a moral obligation to form one's conscience in accordance to right reason and the will of God. It is a life-long task. In the purgative stage of spirituality, the conscience is often poorly formed, while in the succeeding stages the conscience becomes more enlightened. The following are some general guidelines for the proper formation of one's conscience:
- Reflection, self-examination, and introspection make up the ground level of an informed conscience.

---

[57] GS 16; Cf. Rom. 1:32; 2:14-16. All quotes and references from Scripture are from the RSV.
[58] John Henry Newman, "Letter to the Duke of Norfolk," V, in *Certain Difficulties felt by Anglicans in Catholic Teaching* II (London: Longmans Green, 1885), 248.

- Absorption in the Word of God (Ps. 119:105) and Sacred Tradition (the life of the Holy Spirit within the Church) serve as the blood of life for the conscience.
- The authoritative teachings of the Church that flow from Sacred Scripture and Sacred Tradition are essential (cf. 2 Thess. 2: 15).
- Reading the spiritual masters and the advice of good spiritual directors are extremely helpful in putting all the above into a concise vision of reality that corresponds to the innate reality at the core of one's being.

A well-formed conscience engenders freedom and peace of heart.

Determining a Well-Informed Conscience

There are essentially two key guides that help to determine if one has a well-informed conscience:

1) A good end does not justify an evil means.
2) Do unto others as you would like done unto you (cf. Mt. 7:12; Lk. 6:31; Rom. 14:21; 1 Cor. 8:12; Tob. 4:15).

An Uninformed Conscience[59]

> Like all things human, even [the] conscience can fail to...[perceive] illusions and errors. It is a delicate voice that can be overpowered by a noisy, distracted way of life, or almost suffocated by a long-lasting and serious habit of sin.[60]
>
> *Pope John Paul II*

There are two main reasons for an uninformed conscience:

1) The propensity toward laziness is at the heart of those who fail to seek a well-informed conscience.
2) A sinful life often blinds one to recognize the truth and often deadens a person's conscience.

> The more correct conscience prevails, the more do persons and groups turn aside from blind choice and try to be guided by objective standards of moral conduct.[61]
>
> *Gadium et Spes*

---

[59] GS 16.
[60] John Paul II, *Celebrate 2000* (Ann Arbor: Servant Publications, 1996), 151.
[61] GS 16.

An Examination of Conscience

An examination of conscience is a powerful way of keeping one's conscience informed and open to the working of grace.

The following is a general method of examining one's conscience: One must first begin by praying to God for enlightenment. One must then ask oneself the following key questions: "Who am I as God sees me? What is happening in my life at this moment? How is God working in me? How is evil working in me? What is God asking of me? What would Jesus do in my situation?" From these key questions flows a profound examination of conscience.

Original and Personal Sin
Original Sin

> There is nothing upon earth which does not demonstrate either the misery of man or the mercy of God; either the powerlessness of man without God—or his power in union with God.... Man does not know where he belongs. He has obviously gone astray and has fallen from his proper place. He cannot find his way back to it, though he seeks it everywhere in great anxiety but without success, moving about in impenetrable darkness....[62]
>
> *Blaise Pascal*

At the beginning of time humanity had a choice to live with God or live without him (cf. Gen. 3:1-24). The choice to live without God caused a wound, a wound that would forever affect human nature. This wound would come to be known as the *original sin*, a sin of such great nature that it destroyed the possibility of eternal life with God and happiness.

God, in his love, would not allow humanity to remain separated from eternal life with him. He sent his only begotten Son to restore us to new life (2 Cor. 5:17). Sin was forgiven by the merits of Christ.

Concupiscence

Original sin distorted the harmony of creation and damaged the relationship between God and humanity. The second Person of the Trinity, the Son of God, came into the world and cleansed it of this damage, this original sin. While the sin was forgiven in Christ, the wound remained.

---

[62] *The Essential Pascal*, sel. and ed. Robert W. Gleason, S.J., and trans. G.F. Pullen (New York: New American Library, 1966), 69f.

Human beings, in Christ, are capable of an intimate, personal, saving relationship with God, and are capable of experiencing eternal life with God in heaven. Yet despite this, because of the wound of original sin, a human being is still inclined and tempted toward that original rebellion; that is, human beings are inclined toward the temptations of evil.

The spiritual journey is a battle against concupiscence.

Personal Sin

Sin is a personal act in which reason, truth, and right conscience are offended. It is a failure to live up to the command of love of God and neighbor caused by a perverse attachment to that which is not for the honor and glory of God. It is an act of self-infatuation, disobedience (Gen. 3:5) and hatred toward God (Ps. 51:4).[63] It wounds the nature of the human person, the nature of solidarity, and the nature of the eternal law.[64]

Kinds of Sin[65]

Sin comes from the heart, from the very core of a person's being (cf. Mt. 15:19-20). The two main kinds of sins are sins of commission and sins of omission. Sins of commission are sins in which a person takes an active part in—such as in acts of fornication, impurity, licentiousness, idolatry, sorcery, enmity, strife, jealousy, anger, selfishness, dissension, envy, drunkenness, carousing, etc. (cf. Gal 5:19-21; Rom. 1:28-32; 1 Cor. 9-10; Eph. 5:3-5; Col. 3:5-8; 1 Tim. 9-10; 2 Tim. 2-5). Sins of omission are sins that involve actions that are omitted in fostering the glory and honor of God. These are sins committed by people who keep quiet when evil is being done. People who do nothing to put an end to abortion or euthanasia, for example, commit serious sins of omission. Failing to stop gossip, vulgarity, and so forth, are other forms of sins of omission.

Gravity of Sin[66]

> If any one sees his brother committing what is not a mortal sin, he will ask, and God will give him life for those whose sin is not mortal. There is sin which is mortal…. All wrongdoing is sin, but there is sin which is not mortal (2 Jn. 5:16-17).

---

[63] St. Augustine, *De civ. Dei* 14, 28: PL 41, 436.
[64] Ibid., *Contra Faustum* 22: PL 42, 418.
[65] Cf. CCC 1849-1850.
[66] Cf. Ibid., 1854-1864.

There are mortal/deadly sins and there are venial/non-deadly sins. Mortal sins involve the loss of sanctifying grace and love. It is a radical rejection of God, a radical turning away from God. Dying in mortal sin leads to hell. On the other hand, venial or non-deadly sins do not deprive one of heaven. In venial sin love remains, though it is offended and damaged.

In order to commit a mortal sin one needs to take into account the following conditions:

1) The sin must be one that involves a *grave matter*. Traditionally grave matter has been associated with the gross violation of the Ten Commandments.

2) Full knowledge and sufficiently deliberate consent is needed in the committing of a sin.

3) Unintentional ignorance (not feigned ignorance or hardness of heart) diminishes or removes the seriousness of the sin (i.e., pathological disorders, inordinate feelings and passions).

Venial sin is sin that does not meet the above requirements. Venial sin weakens love, disorders affections for created things, hinders virtuous progress, and disposes one toward mortal sin by damaging the conscience. Yet venial sin does not break a person's covenant or friendship with God. It does not deprive one of sanctifying grace nor of heaven.

> While he is in the flesh, man cannot help but have at least some light sins. Despise these sins which we call "light": if you take them for light when you weigh them, tremble when you count them. A number of light objects make a great mass; a number of drops fill a river; a number of grains make a heap. What then is our hope? Above all, confession....[67]
>
> *St. Augustine*

Communal Nature to Spirituality[68]

> An error, "today abundantly widespread, is disregard for the law of human solidarity and charity, dictated and imposed both by our common origin and by the equality in the rational nature of all men, whatever nation they belong to. This law is sealed by the sacrifice of redemption offered by Jesus Christ on the altar on the Cross to his heavenly Father, on behalf of sinful humanity."[69]

---

[67] St. Augustine, *In ep. Jo.* 1, 6: PL 35, 1982.
[68] Cf. CCC 1878-1880; 1928-1942.
[69] Pius XII, *Summi pontificatus*, October 20, 1939; AAS 31 (1939) 423ff.

The love of God and the love of neighbor are inseparable realities. To authentically love God one must authentically love one's neighbor, and to authentically love one's neighbor one needs to authentically love God.

The communal nature of spirituality promotes the common good of society, which promotes the defense of the fundamental rights of persons, the development of spirituality, and peace and security. Any form of sinful inequality is condemned.

Sin and Mercy[70]

All people fall short of the perfection of Christ and therefore sin is a cancer that engulfs this world (cf. 1 Jn. 8-9). Yet despite this sad reality, God's mercy never leaves a person. Even a mortal sin does not withdraw from the core of the person God's divine mercy,[71] for if it did, there would be no possibility of repentance, forgiveness, and conversion.

The Seven Capital Sins and Their Vices

The capital sins are commonly found in the early stages of the spiritual journey. They are often mortal, but not at all times.[72] A person, as a consequence of original sin, is susceptible to capital sins and their vices. A capital sin leads one to separation from God and all kinds of sins. They also lead from lesser sins to more serious sins.

The following is a brief description of the seven capital sins and what is often born of them: The capital sin of envy gives birth to hatred, slander, calumny, detraction, and joy at the misfortune of others. Anger leads to disputes, fits of passion, insults, blasphemy, rudeness, haughtiness and contempt. Vanity leads to disobedience, boasting, hypocrisy, unholy rivalry, discord, and stubbornness. Sloth (or acedia) gives rise to malice, rancor, discouragement, cowardliness, spiritual apathy or stagnation, forgetfulness of spiritual obligations, and the seeking after forbidden things. Avarice gives rise to disloyalty, treachery, fraud, deceit, perjury, harshness, hardness of heart, and an excessive desire for acquiring and maintaining things. Gluttony leads one to engage in improper jokes, coarse, loutish behavior, impurity, foolish conversation, and stupidity. Lust gives rise to spiritual blindness, poor judgment, impetuous or rash decisions, fickleness, instability, capriciousness, self-infatuation, and an inordinate attachment to this present life.[73]

---

[70] Cf. 1846-1848; Cf. Lk. 15.
[71] Ia IIae, q. 88, a.2.
[72] *Dark Night*, BK I, Chs. 2-8.

Prayer in General

> Prayer is the fruit of joy and thanksgiving and the ascent of the person's very being to God. [74]
>
> *Evagrius Ponticus*

> For me prayer is a surge of the heart; it is a simple look turned toward heaven, it is a cry of recognition and of love, embracing both trials and joy. [75]
>
> *St. Therese of Lisieux*

Prayer as gift
"Prayer is the raising of one's mind and heart to God or the requesting of good things from God." [76] Prayer is founded upon humility and a contrite heart (Ps. 130:1; cf. Lk. 18:9-14). One must recognize that one needs help in the endeavor of prayer (Rm. 8:26) and one must recognize that "whether we realize it or not, prayer is an encounter of God's thirst with ours. God thirsts that we may thirst for him" (cf. Jn. 4:10). [77] "Prayer is the response of faith to the free promise of salvation and also a response of love to the thirst of the only Son of God" (cf. Jn. 7:37-39; 19:28; Isa. 12:3; 51:1; Zech. 12:10; 13:1). [78]

Prayer as covenant
When one prays, one prays from the heart, which is the dwelling place where one is, where one lives, where one withdraws to. The heart is

> our hidden center, beyond the grasp of our reason and of others; only the Spirit of God can fathom the human heart and know it fully. The heart is the place of decision, deeper than our psychic drives. It is the place of truth, where we choose life or death. It is the place of encounter, because as image of God we live in relation; it is the place of covenant. [79]

---

[73] Cf. Ia IIae, q. 77, a.4f; q. 84, a.4.
[74] Evagrius Ponticus, *The 153 Chapters on Prayer*, 15, 35.
[75] St. Therese of Lisieux, *Manuscrits autobiographiques*, C 25r.
[76] St. John Damascene, *De fide orth.* 3, 24: PG 94, 1098C; CCC 2559.
[77] Cf. St. Augustine, *De diversis quaestionibu octoginta tribus* 64, 4: PL 40, 56; CCC 2560.
[78] CCC 2561.

Prayer is a committed relationship of life and love. It is meant to be an inseparable relationship of encounter between the Creator and his creation.

Prayer as communion

Prayer is a communion between the individual, God, and his Body the Church. While one may invoke each person of the Trinity and pray to each person of the Trinity, it is traditionally understood that prayer is directed toward the Father, through the Son, and in the Holy Spirit in a mystical community called the Church, the Church on earth, in purgatory, and in heaven. "In the Holy Spirit, Christian prayer is a communion of love with the Father, not only through Christ, but also *in him*..."[80]

Jesus and prayer

Jesus teaches us to pray and reminds us that he prays for us, in us, and with us. As St. Augustine summarizes:

> He prays for us as our priest, prays in us as our Head, and is prayed to by us as our God. Therefore let us acknowledge our voice in him and his in us.[81]

From the *Sermon on the Mount* one is taught that prayer to the Father requires a conversion of the heart. Reconciliation, love of enemies, prayers for persecutors, attentive prayer, purity of heart, and the seeking of the kingdom are all at the core of a conversion of the heart (cf. Mt. 5:23-24, 44-45; 6:7, 14-15, 21, 25, 33).

This conversion of heart leads to praying in faith, an adherence to God beyond what is limited to feelings and understanding. One in faith can therefore be assured of one's access to the Father and the assurance that if one *seeks* and *knocks* one will receive answers, for Christ is the *door* and the *way* (Mt. 7:7-11, 13-14). One can be confident that whatever is asked for in prayer and in faith will be received (Mk. 11:24). One is reminded that in Jesus "all things are possible to him who believes" (Mk. 9:23; cf. Mt. 21:22).

It is important to remember, however, that an authentic prayer of faith is always one that is embodied by a heart disposed to do the will of the Father. Simply crying out "Lord, Lord..." is of little benefit if the heart is far from the will of God (cf. Mt. 7:21). An authentic prayer of faith embodies the divine plan of

---

[79] Ibid., 2563.
[80] Ibid., 2615.
[81] St. Augustine, *En. In Ps.* 85, 1: PL 37, 1081; cf. GILH 7: CCC 2616.

God within it (cf. Mt. 9:38; Lk. 10:2; Jn. 4:34). It realizes the importance of struggle and of patience and perseverance (cf. Lk. 18:1-8). Therefore, prayer is inseparable from works. In the words of Thomas Merton, prayer

> is inseparable from life and from the dynamism of life—which includes work, creation, production, fruitfulness, and above all love.... It is the very fullness of a fully integrated life. It is the crown of life and of all life's activities.[82]

Mary

Mary, Mother of Jesus and of those who participate in his priestly ministry, we come to you with the same attitude of children who come to their mother. We are no longer children, but adults who desire with all our hearts to be God's children. Our human condition is weak; that is why we come to ask for your motherly aid so we are able to overcome our weakness. Pray for us so that we can, in turn, become people of prayer. We invoke your protection so that we may remain free from all sin. We invoke your love so that it may reign and we will be able to be compassionate and forgiving. We ask for your blessing so we can be like the image of your beloved Son, our Lord and Savior, Jesus Christ. Amen.[83]

May the Virgin make our hearts humble and submissive like her son's heart. In her the heart of Jesus was formed. Let us learn to be humble, accepting humiliations with joy. We have been created for great things—why then should we stoop to things that would blur the beauty of our heart? How many things we can learn from the Virgin! Ask the Virgin to tell Jesus, "They have no more wine"—the wine of humility and submission, of goodness, of sweetness.... Ask Jesus to help you personalize your love for Mary—in order to be sources of joy, as he is; in order to be closer to her, as he is; in order to share with her everything, even the cross. Every one of us must carry his or her own cross; it is our sign of belonging to Christ. We need Mary to help us share it.[84]

---

[82] *A Thomas Merton Reader*, Revised Edition. Edited by Thomas O. McDonnell (New York: Image Books, 1974), 400.

[83] Mother Teresa, *In My Own Words: Special Memorial Edition* (Liguori: Liguori Publications, 1996), 61.

[84] Mother Teresa, *Heart of Joy: The Transforming of Self-Giving* (Ann Arbor: Servant Books, 1987),

Mary's intercessory prayers have a unique role in the plan of salvation. At the Annunciation her prayer opened the way for Christ's conception (cf. Lk. 1:38); at Pentecost her prayer helped form the Church (Acts 1:14). In her *fiat*, she was the perfect disciple, the perfect model of the Church; she was what all are called to be: "Behold I am the handmaid of the Lord; let it be [done] to me according to your word" (Lk. 1:38). This is at the heart of Christian prayer: "to be wholly God's, because he is wholly ours."[85]

Mary teaches a person how to pray by her example of humility, love, obedience, faith, and trust.

Mary's intercessory power is unique for she is the Mother of God, the spouse of the Holy Spirit. At the wedding feast of Cana (Jn. 2-12) the wine ran out. Jesus was not prepared to begin his public ministry. Yet when Mary, his mother, asked her Son to help the wedding couple—when Mary interceded—Jesus listened to the intercession of his mother and performed the miracle of turning water into wine. Mary's intercessory power is in her nature as the Mother of the Lord, for what good son can refuse the request of a good mother?

Jesus himself reminds all to have recourse to Mary at the foot of the cross when he turns over to John and the whole world Mary as our Mother, as the New Eve, as the Daughter of Zion, as the Mother of the Church.

> When Jesus saw his mother, and the disciple whom he loved standing near, he said to his mother, "Woman, behold, your son! Then he said to the disciple, "Behold, your mother" (Jn. 19:26)!

Mary is our Mother. Christ gave the world a powerful intercessor for the needs of his people. Christ came into the world through Mary, and one is blessed to go to Jesus through Mary. Because we pray in the power of the Holy Spirit and the Mother of God is the spouse of the Holy Spirit, Mary becomes an essential part in Catholic spirituality.

It is important to recognize that Jesus could have entered the scene of history by simply walking out from the desert without any known origin, yet he chose a mother to enter the world, a mother from whom he took his flesh, a mother whom he listened to and loved. He never ceases to listen to her and to love her.

80-81; 139.
[85] CCC 2617.

Mary never ceases to pray for us, now, and at the hour of our death!

The Church—A Communion

The Scriptures are clear on the necessity of interceding on behalf of others (cf. Lk. 16:9; 1 Cor. 12:12, 20f, 12:26; Heb. 12:22f; Rev. 5:8). The apostles often make reference to the need of praying for others and the need of the prayers of others. God intended this so that people of faith could be members of an authentic community where each member depended on the other, where each member cared for the other, where each member could live out the command of love of neighbor. What a precious act of love it is to pray for one another.

At the heart of this communion is the reality that relationships built on the foundation of grace are relationships that never end. Even death is not the end, nor is it a separation. Quite the contrary, death is simply the beginning of a new phase in eternal life, and in many ways a person who has died is closer to his or her loved ones than ever before. Just as a man or woman loved, cared for, and prayed for his or her loved ones on this earthly journey, they do the same in heaven, but in a much more powerful way. For the person who is in heaven is a person who dwells in the sphere of perfection and thus is a person who has been cleansed and purified of all his or her imperfections and sins (2 Macc. 12:46f). The powerful prayers of the pure of heart cannot be denied.

Whether from earth or from heaven, we pray as a community of faith, as the Church.

Expressions of Prayer

Vocal Prayer

Vocal prayer is a form of prayer that lays the groundwork and nourishes all other forms of prayer. As vocal prayer progresses it opens one's being for the higher forms of prayer.[86] Vocal prayer is the initial form of contemplative prayer.[87]

Vocal prayer is the incarnation of a person's heart's interaction with God. Words bring flesh to prayer. Human nature demands that one's whole body participate in the worship of God--body, soul, and spirit. Prayer is the worship of God with one's whole being (cf. Mt. 11:25-26; Mk. 14:36).

Meditation

---

[86] *Way*, Ch. 25.
[87] CCC 2702.

What is meditating on Christ? It is simply this, thinking habitually and constantly of Him and of His deeds and sufferings. It is to have Him before our minds as One whom we may [reflect upon], worship, and address when we rise up, when we lie down, when we eat and drink, when we are at home and abroad, when we are working, or walking, or at rest, when we are alone, and again when we are in company; this is meditating. And by this, and nothing short of this, will our hearts come to feel as they ought.[88]

John Henry Newman

For the Carthusian monk, Guigo II, "meditation is the busy application of the mind to seek with the help of one's own reason the knowledge of hidden truth."[89] Meditation in a most profound way moves a person away from unhealthy, "worldly" things.[90]

Meditation is the seeking of the life of God. The mind seeks to search out the mystery of life in meditation. Through Sacred Scripture, Sacred Tradition, spiritual books, sacred icons, liturgical texts and seasons as well as through history and creation one encounters many answers to the mystery of life. One also encounters the path that one must travel.

Meditation makes a person encounter his or her deepest self. The book of life is opened to be explored. In this exploration one asks: "Lord, what do you want me to do?" Meditation helps one to be well grounded in the life of Christ (cf. Mk. 4:4-7; 15-19).

Meditation eventually will transform itself into contemplation, the only means for complete union with God.[91] As the *Catechism* states:

Meditation engages thought, imagination, emotion, and desire. This mobilization of faculties is necessary in order to deepen our convictions of faith, prompt the conversion of our heart, and strengthen our will to follow Christ. Christian prayer tries above all to meditate on the mysteries of Christ, as in the *lectio divina* or the rosary. This form of prayerful reflection is of a great value, but Christian prayer should go further: to the knowledge of the love of the Lord Jesus, to union with him.[92]

---

[88] John Henry Newman, *Parochial and Plain Sermons* (London: Longman, Green, and Co., 1910) VI, 41.

[89] *Guigo II: The Ladder of Monks: A Letter on the Contemplative Life and Twelve Meditations*, trans. Edmund College, OSB, and James Walsh, S.J. (Kalamazoo: Cistercian Publications, 1981), 68.

[90] *Living Flame*, St. 3, no. 32; *Ascent*, BK III, Ch. 15, no. 2.

[91] *Ascent*, BK II, Ch. 16, no. 7.

> Contemplative prayer in my opinion is nothing else than a close sharing between friends; it means taking time frequently to be alone with him who we know loves us.[93]
>
> *St. Teresa of Avila*

Contemplation is the quest for the one "whom my soul loves" (Song of Songs 1:7; cf. 3:1-4). One enters this form of prayer in quiet, poverty, and pureness of faith. One seeks to be offered up to God in this experience; one seeks to be purified and transformed into the image and likeness one was meant to be transformed into; that is, in the image and likeness of Jesus Christ. Contemplation is love welcoming love (cf. Lk. 7:36-50; 19:1-10). It is victory in the total surrendering. In contemplation the "Father strengthens our inner being with power through his Spirit so 'that Christ may dwell in [our] hearts through faith' and we may be 'grounded in love'" (Eph. 3:16-17).[94]

Contemplation is the entrance into the sphere of the experience of God which transcends the limits of anything we hear, see, touch, smell, imagine, etc. It is beyond the limits of the internal and external senses. The God who transcends all speaks in silence to the heart of the person engaged in contemplation. He speaks with a presence of such intensity that the senses are incapable of grasping the fullness of this presence.

> The spirit helps us...for we do not know how to pray as we ought; but the Spirit himself makes intercession for us with groanings that cannot be expressed in speech (cf. Rom. 8:26).

Aspects of Prayer
Blessing

Blessing exemplifies the basic movement of prayer. When one prays, one is praying in an ascending order. One prays in the power of the Holy Spirit, through the Son, to the Father. In such a fashion one can be said to be blessing God who is the source of all blessings (cf. Eph. 1:3-14; 2 Cor. 1:3-7; 1 Pet. 1:3-9). Through the grace of the Holy Spirit that descends through the Son and from the Father one is in turn blessed from the source of all blessings (cf. 2 Cor. 13:14; Rm. 15:5-6; Eph. 6:23-24). Because "God blesses, the human heart can

---

[92] CCC 2708.
[93] *The Book of Her Life*, 8, 5.
[94] CCC 2714.

in return bless the One who is the source of every blessing."[95] To bless is to make another happy!

Adoration

Adoration is an act of humility, the doorway to holiness. In an act of adoration a person makes himself or herself aware that he or she is a created being in the presence of an almighty, omniscient Creator (cf. Ps. 95:1-6). Adoration is the realization that one has been saved by a Savior, by the King of all kings. It is the recognition that one has been set free from the slavery of sin to be a child of God (cf. Ps. 24:9-10).

Petition

Through one's petitions to God one is making present, in the most obvious of ways, the reality that one is in a relationship with God. In the act of asking, beseeching, pleading, invoking, entreating, and crying out to God one is showing one's need and love for God (cf. Rm. 15:30; Col. 4:12). A petition is an acknowledgement that one is a sinner in need of a savior. It is an act of turning toward God (cf. Rm. 8:22-24, 26). Prayers of petition require the awareness that one is in need of forgiveness (cf. Lk. 18:13) and that one is in need of the gifts of humility and trust (cf. 1 Jn. 1:7-2:2; 3:22).

Intercessions

An intercessory prayer is a unique form of a prayer of petition. It is closely modeled on Jesus' prayers. While it is true that Jesus is the one intercessor (cf. Rm. 8:34; 1 Jn. 2:1; 1 Tim. 2:5-8; Heb. 7:25), Jesus has granted the gift to all in grace to intercede in him, with him, and through him (cf. Lk. 23:28, 34; Rm. 8:26-27; 10:1; 12:14; Acts 7:60; 12:5; 20:36; 21:5; Eph. 6:18-20; 2 Cor. 9:14; Phil. 1:3-4; 2:4; 1 Thess. 5:25; 2 Thess. 1:11; Col. 1:3; 4:3-4; 1 Tim. 2:1). A person of faith is a member of a community of love, the Church, the Body, the Bride of Christ (cf. Col. 1:24; 2 Cor. 11:2). As a consequence each member is to help the other members. Each member is called to love the other members. But God demands even more; he calls one to love even those who are outside the boundaries of the mystical Body. One must also pray for persecutors and all enemies of the Gospel (cf. Lk. 6:35).

Thanksgiving

One gives thanks to God for being freed from sin and slavery. One gives thanks for the gift of grace, the gift of eternal life with God. One gives thanks

---

[95] Ibid., 2626.

for being made a *new creation* in Christ (cf. 2 Cor. 5:17). Because of the precious gift of immortality, because of all God's precious gifts, every event in one's life, even the most difficult, the most painful, are worthy of thanksgiving. As St. Paul states: "Give thanks in all circumstances; for this is the will of God in Christ Jesus for you" (1 Thess. 5:18). In the mystery that is life, even the most hideous of circumstances can be transformed into a gift. Within the mystery of suffering is the mystery of love, and within the mystery of love is the mystery of suffering.

Praise

When one praises God one is worshipping God for simply being God. One is not focused on God's gifts, his "goodies," but simply on God. One praises God because *HE IS*. It is the prayer of the pure of heart and consequently it is the prayer that embraces all other prayers (cf. Rm. 8:16; 16:25-27; 1 Cor. 8:6; Acts 2:47; 3:9; 4:21; 13:48; Eph. 1:3-14, 20-21; 5:14, 19; Col. 1:15-20; 3:16; Phil. 2:6-11; 1 Tim. 3:16; 6:15-16; 2 Tim. 2:11-13; Jude 24-25; Jas. 1:17; Rev. 4:8-11; 5:9-14; 6:10; 7:10-12).

The Battle of Prayer

Prayer is a gift that requires grace. Prayer is always brought about by an act of God. A person's part in the experience of prayer is to respond to this initiative. One must remember that even before one can cry out to God, God is already there initiating that cry.

Prayer is a battle because it is a struggle against the consequences of original sin, concupiscence, and the temptations of the devil. Time constraints, the inability to experience or understand the supernatural, a preoccupation with sensuality, the sense that prayer is an escape rather than an encounter, the sense of discouragement, dryness, wounded pride, sin, and so forth all have an impact on a person's ability to pray. What is required of the person is a response, in grace, to the battle with the armaments of humility, trust, and perseverance.[96]

The battle in prayer is extremely important for a person's spiritual growth, for the wounds of the battle help one see where one is on this spiritual road. One is able to see if one is closer to victory or defeat by observing one's wounds. For example, distractions in prayer help one to see what one is attached to, which master one serves (cf. Mt. 6:21, 24). Is one vigilant in the battle or has one become lax (cf. Mt. 26:41)? Dryness in prayer can tell one whether one is being asked to walk by faith or if one is being asked to repent

---

[96] Ibid., 2726-2728.

and turn back to God; in other words, is the dryness due to progress in holiness or is it due to sinfulness? Does distress help one to trust more or does it lead to despair (cf. Rm. 5:3-5)? Prayers that seem not to be answered can clarify one's motives in prayer: Does one love God as an instrument of selfishness or as a God who deserves love for simply being God?

In Summary

Prayer is not the manipulating of God to acquire something that God did not know we needed; quite the contrary, God knows all, including our needs. He knows what we will ask and all the free will decisions we will make in advance. He knows what we need and how it fits within his providence--that sphere of representativeness that is between two extremes, predestination and absolute, undeterred free will.

Why pray if God is all knowing? We pray to show our need, our love, and our dependence upon God, not because God needs this love or dependence, but because we do. We pray because it teaches us about ourselves and our priorities? We pray because it develops our spiritual brain, and thus brings light, happiness, and peace into our life and world.

Atheists often argue against the belief in God because answered prayers are not provable objectively. Prayer, unfortunately for the atheist, is not so simplistic a concept.

For the believer prayers are answered, but not necessarily in the manner in which one expects the prayer to be answered. Prayers are answered in such a fashion that one's eternal destiny is always in the forefront. Prayer is always answered with the understanding that this earthly life is but a blink of the eye when compared to eternity. Prayer is always understood from the perspective of the present and future good of the world and with the understanding that all prayers are interconnected—at the level of the individual, the community, and the world.

When we look upon the history of our prayers and desires, we see that our prayers were in fact answered, but most often in ways we did not expect. This is beautifully illustrated in the words of an unknown civil war soldier:

> I asked for strength that I might achieve; I was made weak that I might learn humbly to obey. I asked for health that I might do greater things; I was given infirmity that I might do better things. I asked for riches that I might be happy; I was given poverty that I might be wise. I asked for power that I might have the praise of men; I was given weakness that I might feel the need of God. I asked for all things that I might enjoy life; I was given life that I might enjoy all things. I got

nothing that I asked for, but everything that I had hoped for. Almost despite myself, my unspoken prayers were answered; I am, among all men, most richly blessed.

In humility, trust and perseverance all prayers are heard.
The sense of unanswered prayers can often lead to the abandonment of the spiritual life. Thus, the love-driven gifts of humility and trust are so important for they empower the love-driven gift of perseverance that is essential for any battle (cf. 1 Thess. 5:17; Eph. 5:20; 6:8).
Victory leads to enlightenment, peace and happiness. Defeat leads to slavery (cf. Gal. 5:16-25).

Sacraments

For the Catholic sacraments are efficacious and therefore essential for growth in holiness. Sacraments produce what they signify. A sacrament imparts grace to the individual (Acts 2:38; 8:17; 19:4-7; 1 Pet. 3:19-22).[97] Thus, a person's disposition on receiving the sacraments has a great impact on his or her holiness.[98]

Baptism[99]

Baptism regenerates us in the life of the Son of God; unites us to Christ and to His Body, the Church; it anoints us in the Holy Spirit, making us spiritual temples.[100]

Pope John Paul II

Baptism is a sacrament with real power and it is a sacrament that is necessary for salvation, for it is by baptism that we are "born again" of *water* and the *Spirit* (Jn. 3:5; Mk. 16:16). In baptism one enters into Christ's death and resurrection (cf. Rom. 6:3-4). One has put on Christ in baptism (Gal. 3:27). Baptism cleanses one from original sin, personal sin, and the punishment for sin (Mk. 16:16; Jn. 3:5; Acts 2:38f; 22:16; Rom. 6:3-6; Gal. 3:7; 1 Cor. 6:11; Eph. 5:26; Col. 2:12-14; Heb. 10:22). One becomes a new creation in Christ and a partaker in the divine nature (2 Pet. 1:4). One becomes a member of the Church as an adopted child of God (cf. 1 Cor. 12-13; 27). One becomes a

---

[97] Cf. Ibid., 1076-1130; 1210-1211.
[98] Cf. IIIa, q. 89, a.2.
[99] Cf. CCC 1213-1274.
[100] John Paul II, *Celebrate 2000: Reflections on Jesus, the Holy Spirit, and the Father* (Ann Arbor: Servant Publications, 1996), 40.

Temple of the Holy Spirit (Acts 2:38; 19:5f) with an indelible mark or character on the soul which enables one to share in the priesthood of Christ and in his passion (Mk. 10:38f; Lk. 12:50).

Confirmation[101]

Confirmation perfects baptismal grace. Once confirmed one is strengthened by the Holy Spirit to be a powerful witness of Christ's self-communicating love to the world. One becomes a strengthened member in the mission of the Church, the proclamation of the Gospel. Like baptism, a sacred mark or seal is imprinted on the soul, forever changing it. In receiving this sacrament by a bishop or a delegated priest, one is making a commitment to profess the faith and to serve the world in word and deed as a disciple of Christ (Acts 19:5-6; 8:16-17; Heb. 6:1-2; 2 Cor. 1:21-22; Eph. 1:13).

The Eucharist[102]

St. Justin Martyr, in the year 150 AD, some fifty years after the death of the last apostle John, wrote to the Emperor Antoninus Pius regarding the long-standing practice of early Christian worship:

> On the day we call the day of the sun, all who dwell in the city or country gather in the same place.
> The memoirs of the apostles and the writings of the prophets are read, as much as time permits.
> When the reader has finished, he who presides over those gathered admonishes and challenges them to imitate these beautiful things.
> Then we all rise together and offer prayers* for ourselves...and for all others, wherever they may be, so that we may be found righteous by our life and actions, and faithful to the commandments, so as to obtain eternal salvation.
> When the prayers are concluded we exchange the kiss. Then someone brings bread and a cup of water and wine mixed together to him who presides over the brethren.
> He takes them and offers praise and glory to the Father of the universe, through the name of the Son and of the Holy Spirit and for a considerable time he gives thanks (in Greek: *eucharistian*) that we have been judged worthy of these gifts.

---

[101] Cf. CCC 1285-1314.
[102] Cf. Ibid., 1322-1405.

When he has concluded the prayers and thanksgiving, all present give voice by an acclamation by saying: 'Amen.'
When he who presides has given thanks and the people have responded, those whom we call deacons give to those present the "eucharisted" bread, wine, and water and take them to those who are absent.[103]

In explaining the mystery indicated by the word "eucharisted," Justin states in his *First Apology*:

We call this food Eucharist...since Jesus Christ our Savior was made incarnate by the word of God and had both flesh and blood for our salvation, so too, as we have been taught, the food which has been made into the Eucharist by the Eucharistic prayer set down by Him, and by the change of which our blood and flesh is nourished, is both the flesh and the blood of that incarnated Jesus.[104]

The Eucharist is the real presence of Christ--his real glorified, resurrected body and blood (Mt. 26:26-28; Mk. 14:22-24; Lk. 22:19f; Jn. 6:51f; 1 Cor. 10:16; 11:24f).

The Eucharist is the "source and summit of our faith." All things flow from the Eucharist and return back to it.

The Mass is the *re-presenting*, or making present of what took place once and for all at Calvary (Heb. 7:27; 9:12, 25-28; 10:10-14). Just as the Passover meal made present to those who participated in it the Exodus events, the Mass in a fuller way makes present what happened at Calvary. At every Mass, Calvary is made present to all. Mass is a participation in that one and only sacrifice on the cross at Calvary (cf. Heb. 7:27).

The Eucharist is the "medicine of immortality, the antidote that we should not die, but live in Jesus forever."[105] The Eucharist increases a person's union with the Lord, forgives venial sins, and preserves that person from grave sin. By the fact that it strengthens the individual, it consequently strengthens the unity of the Church as Christ's mystical Body.

...and having received the Food that gives life immediately after the procession, I thought only of God and myself; and I beheld my soul,

---

[103] *Apol.* 65-67; PG 6, 428-429.
[104] St. Justin Martyr, *First Apology*, 66, quoted in William Jurgens, *The Faith of the Early Fathers*, vol. 1 (Collegeville: The Liturgical Press, 1970), 55.
[105] Ignatius of Antioch, trans. Lake (Cambridge: Harvard University Press, 1998), *Ephesians*, 20.

under the similitude of wax softened by the fire, impressed like a
seal upon the bosom of the Lord....[106]

St Gertrude the Great

Reconciliation/Penance[107]

The forgiveness of serious sin, or what we call mortal/deadly sin (1 Jn.
5:17) requires the authority of the priest as an authoritative, power-filled
representative of God and of the community. When one looks at the Scriptures
(Mt. 16:19; 18:18; Jn. 20:21-23) it becomes obvious that God entrusted his
apostles with the gift of forgiving sins.

Jesus has an important reason for giving the world the Sacrament of
Penance. When one sins one harms one's relationship with God, with the
community, and one does damage to one's own being. That is because
through sin one breaks the two commandments that God placed side by side,
the love of God and the love of neighbor as oneself (Mt. 22:37-40).

The spiritual effects of the Sacrament of Penance are beautifully
summarized in the *Catechism of the Catholic Church* (1496):

--reconciliation with God by which the penitent recovers grace;
--reconciliation with the Church;
--remission of eternal punishment incurred by mortal sins;
--remission, at least in part, of temporal punishments resulting from sin;
--peace and serenity of conscience, and spiritual consolation;
--an increase of spiritual strength for the Christian battle.

Anointing of the Sick[108]

Are any among you sick? Let him call for the [priests] of the church,
and let them pray over him, anointing him with oil in the name of
the Lord; and the prayer of faith will save the sick man, and the Lord
will raise him up; and if he has committed sins, he will be forgiven
(Jas. 5:14-15).

This sacrament confers special grace on those suffering from illness or old
age. It is a sacrament that can only be administered by a bishop or a priest. Its

---

[106] *The Life and Revelations of Saint Gertrude, Virgin and Abbess of the Order of St. Benedict*, trans.
M.F.C. Cusak (Westminster: Christian Classics, 1983), 87f.
[107] Cf. CCC 1422-1470.
[108] Cf. CCC 1499-1525.

power is in the unifying of a person's sufferings with the Passion of Christ. It brings God's healing and loving presence upon the person. At times the healing is spiritual, and at times it is emotional or physical. God brings about what is best for a person's eternal destiny, his or her salvation. If a person is unable to receive the Sacrament of Penance it forgives the sins of the person (Mk. 6:12-13; Jas. 5:13-15).

Matrimony[109]

> How can I ever express the happiness of a marriage joined by the Church, strengthened by an offering, sealed by a blessing, announced by angels, and ratified by the Father? How wonderful the bond between two believers, now one in hope, one in desire, one in discipline, one in the same service! They are both children of one Father and servants of the same Master, undivided in spirit and flesh, truly two in one flesh. Where the flesh is one, one also is the spirit.[110]
>
> *Tertullian*

Christ elevated marriage to the level of a sacrament by the gift of grace. The reality of a man who gives himself completely, without doubt, without reservation, fully to his wife, and a wife who gives herself completely, without doubt, fully to her husband can only come about by the supernatural gift of grace. It is only in this way that two can really become one (Mt. 19:3-6; Mk. 10:6-9). Because of this unity to which God calls a couple, marriage must be holy, indissoluble, and open to life (1 Thess. 4:4; 1 Tim. 2:15). Marriage must mirror Christ's love for his own Bride, the Church (Eph. 5:25, 32-32). It mirrors God's covenant with his people. Marriage is, therefore, that which must be blessed by the Church.

Holy Orders[111]

The Sacrament of Holy Orders is an indispensable part of the Church. Without it the Church would not be able to trace itself back to apostolic times, and therefore back to Christ.

The Church makes a distinction between the common priesthood of all the faithful (1 Pet. 2:9) and the ordained priesthood. All Christians are called to be a priestly people, a healing, loving, forgiving people, but some of the faithful are specifically set aside by Jesus for unique ministerial roles. The priesthood

---

[109] Cf. Ibid., 1601-1658.
[110] *Ad uxorem*, 2, 8, 6-7: PL 1, 1412-1413.
[111] Cf. CCC 1536-1600.

conferred by the Sacrament of Holy Orders is one that is specifically designated for teaching, leading worship, and meeting the pastoral needs of the people. Holy Orders are directed toward the holiness of the people of God.

The most important of the Holy Orders is that of the bishop because he serves as the visible head of the local or particular Church. Every bishop in the world can trace himself back in time to an apostle. Bishops have the fullness of the priesthood and are crucial in protecting the true faith. The preeminent of the bishops is of course the Pope, since he is the successor of the leader of the apostles, Peter.

The next order is the presbyter or what we commonly call the priest. He is a "prudent-coworker" and extension of the bishop. He receives his authority from the bishop, and teaches in power because of his tie to the tree of apostolic succession.

The final order is that of the deacon who likewise is attached to the bishop, but who is entrusted primarily with works of charity.

Holy Orders were instituted by Christ (Lk. 22:19; Jn. 20:22f), conferred by the imposition of hands by an apostle or his successor (Acts 6:6; 13:3; 14:23) and give grace (1 Tim. 4:14; 2 Tim. 1:6-7).

Holy Orders are at the service of the people of God, bringing Christ's gift of grace to the journeying faithful.

In Conclusion

In order to grasp the nature of the spiritual journey, one needs to grasp the foundational aspects that propel this journey. As we proceed to the traditional stages of the spiritual journey it will be essential to keep in mind what has been discussed in this foundational chapter.

III
The Purgative Stage
The Age of the Superficial

May the Lord Jesus touch our eyes, as he did those of the blind. Then we shall begin to see in visible things those which are invisible. May he open our eyes to gaze, not on present realities, but on the blessings to come. May he open the eyes of our heart to contemplate God in Spirit, through Jesus Christ the Lord, to whom belong power and glory through all eternity.

Origen

The Pillars of Holiness

Humility

> Humility is the first entry into religion, as it was Christ's first step into the world.... Humility has always been the cornerstone to sanctity....[112]
>
> *Francisco de Osuna*

Humility is the doorway to holiness, for it is the doorway to true self-knowledge. It is important to realize that humility is not low self-esteem, rather it is the recognition that all of one's gifts are from God. Humility is just another name for self-knowledge—that ability to know ourselves the way God truly knows us. Humility avoids unnecessary and unworthy praise, self-seeking, the impressing of others or boasting, and the pursuit of worldly "things" such as fame. Humility promotes the awareness of the need for growth through the recognition of one's weaknesses and sins. It acknowledges the need for compassion, assistance and strength. It promotes a clear conscience and the strength to bear the cross. It rejoices in being corrected and sees reproaches as kisses from God. Humility helps one to be a person for others and recognizes that all things and activities are to be for the glory and honor of God, and that all of life is part of God's providential plan.[113]

Love[114]

God is love and whoever does not know love does not know God (cf. 1 Jn. 4:7). The guiding force of grace is love, for one always moves toward what one loves. Without love, outward deeds are of little significance. On the other hand, to love much is to authentically do much. Love makes one pure of heart: it makes what one appears outwardly the reality of what one is inwardly. In love all is done for the honor and glory of God. Love makes a person seek to turn all things to good. Love never seeks to justify or rationalize the evil one has done. Love makes one never long for special attention or affection to the exclusion of others. In love one recognizes the inseparable nature of the love of God and the love of neighbor. Any authentic love of God requires an authentic love of neighbor and any authentic love of neighbor requires an authentic love of God. Love makes one acknowledge that if one seeks forgiveness one must be

---

[112] *Francisco de Osuna: The Third Spiritual Alphabet*, trans. and intro. Mary E. Giles (Mahwah: Paulist Press, 1981), 494f.

[113] Thomas a Kempis, *Imitation of Christ*, BK I, 2, 3, 7; BK II, 2, 4, 5, 12; BK III, 17, 20, 22, 24, 29, 35-36, 46, 50, 54.

[114] Ibid., BK I, 15, 19, 24; BK II, 3, 5, 8; BK III, 35.

forgiving. Love makes a person look at the best in others. It is not suspicious of anyone.

> Love is patient and kind; love is not jealous or boastful; it is not arrogant or rude. Love does not insist on its own way; it is not irritable or resentful; it does not rejoice at wrong, but rejoices in the right. Love bears all things, believes all things, hopes all things, endures all things. Love never ends (1 Cor. 13:4-8).

Silence

The spiritual journey requires an openness to silence, to calm (cf. Ps. 62:1). Silence allows a person to be open to God's will and therefore is a must in a person's spiritual journey. Silence allows one to read, reflect, meditate, and pray in an authentic manner. It allows one to spend time with God and learn from him. A person who talks too much is a person who knows too little. Silence permits growth in intimacy with God, for God speaks in the silence. Silence affords the opportunity for one to be prepared for work, for proclaiming the Gospel to the ends of the world. Silence helps one act prudently in one's work. It promotes sincere repentance and contrition. It promotes the recognition of one's sinfulness and allows one to search the depths of one's conscience. Silence promotes humility, love, mortification, and the seeking of truth. It recognizes the emptiness of "worldly" things. It allows one to experience peace of mind and to rest in the Lord. It keeps one focused on death, on one's eternal destiny, on one's purpose and meaning in life.[115]

Hunger for Truth

God is truth, and since he is truth, the spiritual path must be a quest for truth (cf. Jn. 4:24). Truth helps one seek to follow right reason and an informed conscience. It aids one to affirm the imperfections of human knowledge and thus the need for the correcting power of divine revelation. The hunger for truth helps one seek the advice of holy and learned people, and the advice of the saints and the Fathers of the Church. Truth grants one the gift of thinking about what is being said and not in who is saying it. One becomes cautious in what is being portrayed as truth. One sifts and distinguishes the good from the evil. The hunger for truth helps one experience life in authentic freedom. Often the devil makes what is evil seem very appealing in order to enslave a person. The hunger for truth helps one to seek beyond what one experiences

---

[115] Ibid., BK I, 24-25.

through the senses. Truth opens the heart and guides one to discover the God who is within and helps one to seek all that is necessary for salvation.[116]

Mortification and Detachment

> Love is a good disposition of the soul by which one prefers no being to the [experience] of God. It is impossible to reach the habit of this love if one has any attachments to earthly things.[117]
>
> *St. Maximus Confessor*

> Jesus has many lovers of his heavenly kingdom, but few cross-bearers.[118]
>
> *Thomas a Kempis*

> If God in His love for the human race had not given us tears, those being saved would be few indeed and hard to find....[119] Tears come from nature, from God, from suffering good and bad, from vainglory, from licentiousness, from love, from the remembrance of death, and from numerous other causes.... Tears can wash away sins as water washes away something written. And as some, lacking water, use other means to wipe off what is written, souls lacking tears beat and scour away their sins with grief, groans, and deep sorrow....[120]
>
> *St. John Climacus*

A person's passions, his or her affections or feelings, can help a person in seeking the good and avoiding the evil. Among the primary passions that affect a person are love, hatred, fear, joy, sadness, and anger. In and of themselves, feelings, affections, or emotions are neither good nor evil. They are neutral. It is what one does with these passions that can cause spiritual harm. In other words, if the feeling of love is picked up by the virtue of justice, one is likely to be merciful in the carrying out of justice. If, however, the feeling of love is picked up by a vice, such as lust, then authentic love becomes perverted. If the passions are in order with right reason and good will, then they are beneficial in

---

[116] Ibid., BK I, 2, 5; BK II, 45; BK III 4, 50.

[117] *Maximus Confessor: Selected Writings*, trans. George C. Berthold (Mahwah: Paulist Press, 1985), n. 1.

[118] Thomas a Kempis, *The Imitation of Christ*, BK II, Ch. 11.

[119] *John Climacus: The Ladder of Divine Ascent*, trans. Colm Luibheid and Norman V. Russell (Mahwah: Paulist Press, 1982), 137.

[120] Ibid., 139-140, 259.

the spiritual life, particularly in the early purgative stages. If these passions, however, are contrary to right reason and the proper use of the will, then they are the source of self-destruction and slavery (cf. Jn. 8:34).[121]

Detachment involves a healthy indifference to worldly concerns. By being detached of all one can love all authentically, the way God intended all to be loved. One seeks to be detached of all that is not for the glory and honor of God; on the other hand, *one is called to be attached to all that is for the glory and honor of God*. Mortification involves the denial of the passions and appetites in order to purify them and in order to purify one's direction toward God. Detachment and mortification are both essential aspects of the spiritual life for they help one to empty the self of all that is not of God. They are lessons in self-mastery, which is at the heart of holiness and happiness.

One is called through detachment and mortification to lead a life of obedience, self-discipline and simplicity. One is called to avoid vanity and pride and the propensity for lying and gossiping, which are signs of self-infatuation. A person must be aware of deceptive and inordinate pleasures which are momentary, but that in the long run lead to sadness and remorse. An individual must seek the best in people and fight off the innate inclination to see the worst in them. One must seek to uncover in others the image of Christ to love, and one must seek to model one's life after Christ's. A person must avoid trying to see his or her self as always better than others. One must be able to realize that others are often better in many ways. A person must avoid criticizing and judging others, for people are so often mistaken in their assessments of others and therefore offend God. People often judge according to their emotions and their self-will and stubbornness. They often judge with poorly formed, self-seeking opinions. Bearing the defects of others in patience and praying for their holiness is precious. It is so easy to fall into the trap of seeking perfection in others but refusing to see the imperfections in our very nature.

One must seek the submission of one's will to God's by being faithful to Scripture, Sacred Tradition, and the teachings of the Church and its authoritative leadership. One must seek to conform one's will to God's and not the other way around. A person must do, at times, what he or she doesn't want to do and to leave undone what he or she would like to do. An individual is called to rejoice in adversity, in not having his or her way. Not having one's way purifies one in order to put one's hope in God and not in "worldly" things.

---

[121] St. Augustine, *De civ. Dei*, 14, 7, 2: PL 41, 410; Ia IIae, q. 24, a.1, 3.

A person must seek devout conversations and delve into all aspects of the spiritual life. One must, consequently, avoid "worldly" people for they lead one into dangerous waters.

A person must resist temptation by turning to God immediately. By doing so the person becomes humble, clean, and learned. However, given the reality of unavoidable temptations, one must take the opportunity to grow through times of temptation. A person's response to temptation shows that person who he or she truly is.

A person must continually seek to repent and experience sorrow for sin. A person must keep his or her eye continually on death by acts of meditation. A person is called to embrace suffering as a precious gift that purifies that person of all that is not of God. One must pray that one does not find too much consolation, for too much consolation can lead to sins of presumption and pride. One must unite one's sufferings to Christ's patiently, willingly, and without complaint. One must not seek so much rest as patience and endurance on this earthly journey.

All things and all works must be directed toward God for happiness. Anything not directed toward God is earthbound and ultimately a disappointment. One must find comfort in the reality that from all eternity God knew the path one would take and that God would always be there to meet one's deepest needs. A person must remember that all "things" are part of God's providential plan. Nothing happens by chance.[122]

Surrender and Trust

Total abandonment consists of giving oneself fully to God because God has given himself to us. If God, who owes us nothing, is willing to give us nothing less than himself, can we respond by giving him only a part of ourselves?

...Jesus wants us to put all our trust in him. We have to renounce our desires in order to work for our own perfection. Even if we feel like a boat without a compass on the high seas, we are to commit ourselves fully to him, without trying to control his actions.

I cannot long for a clear perception of my progress along the route, nor long to know precisely where I am on the path of holiness.

---

[122] *Imitation of Christ*, BK I, 3-14; 16; 20-23; BK II, 2, 10; BK III, 9, 13, 15, 19, 20, 22, 24, 31, 35, 37-39, 46-50, 54.

I ask Jesus to make me a saint. I leave it to him to choose the means that can lead me in that direction.[123]

Mother Teresa

Life is an adventure in which God is in control. God's providential will cannot be thwarted. Any attempt at thwarting God's will always leads to disappointments, anxieties, and every other kind of unhappiness one can imagine. Only in God's will is there rest (Ps. 62:2). Only in God's will is there peace and happiness.

The key to life is surrendering to God's will and trusting that he will take one to that place which is best for one's soul. Life must be experienced as an adventure: Every morning one must wake up and say: "Lord, what adventure do you have planned for me today? Will it be a joyous one or will it be a hard and difficult one? In any case, I'm ready for the adventure and I joyously take it on, for I know you are in control and that you will never abandon me! I surrender and I trust, for in surrendering and trusting I find the victory of my life."

Surrendering and trusting in God is a life-long process, but it is the only process that can lead one to peace and contentment as well as purpose and meaning.

Predominant Inclinations and Faults

> People are often unreasonable and self-centered. Forgive them anyway. If you are kind, people may accuse you of ulterior motives. Be kind anyway. If you are honest, people may cheat you. Be honest anyway. If you find happiness, people may be jealous. Be happy anyway. The good you do today may be forgotten tomorrow. Do good anyway. Give the world the best you have and it may never be enough. Give your best anyway. For you see, in the end, it is between you and God. It was never between you and them anyway.
>
> Mother Teresa

All persons have a predominant fault or faults (cf. 2 Cor. 12:7). A predominant fault is a weakness that one bears as a consequence of one's natural temperament (or as a consequence of the development of a pathological disorder). Predominant faults tend to be troubling to the spiritual journey. Predominant faults have a powerful effect on one's feelings, judging,

---

[123] Mother Teresa, *Heart of Joy*, 125-126.

willing, acting, and so forth. They can at times be hidden and at times disguised as a virtue (i.e., poor self-esteem as humility). They can at times be sinless or at times be the source of a great many sins.

In the *purgative stage* of spirituality there is the beginning of a process of enlightenment: the old self is coming into conflict with the new self. The old way of life is now being replaced with a new way of life, a way that is happier and more productive. This *new self* becomes more and more new and healthy as it discards all that is negative in the old self and keeps all that is positive of the old self. Christ, the *Great Physician* (cf. Mk. 2:17), is beginning to open the eyes of the individual in ways that were never open before. One's life is beginning to be enlightened in ways never before and God is now challenging the person to change for the better. This revolutionary process, which begins the purgative stage, will grow to its ultimate fruition through the illuminative stage and into the unitive stage.[124]

It is important that in discussing the above predominate inclinations and faults, that one remember that in the spiritual person all of the theological virtues, the cardinal and capital virtues, and all the gifts of the Spirit are active. It is simply that some are more obviously active than others. Furthermore, as one progresses in the spiritual journey, the gifts and virtues become less and less hampered by the taint of sin and thus the fruits of the life of grace, such as charity, joy, peace, patience, benignity, goodness, longanimity, mildness, faith, modesty, continency, and chastity, flow more profusely and significantly.

The Blind Side

All people have a blind side; that is, a side to their personality that most people are able to spot, except for the person experiencing this blind spot. People can be egotistical, gossipers, compulsive manipulators and liars, vengeful, lacking self-esteem, etc., and not be in the least bit aware of these realities. Everyone around them, for the most part recognize the blindness, but they themselves are completely oblivious.

All people have various blind spots. The key to the spiritual life is being open to discovering these blind spots.

Blind spots are brought to light through all the gifts and virtues, but particularly the gifts of wisdom, understanding, and knowledge, and the capital virtue of humility. Through these gifts and in particular the infused gift of

---

[124] Part of the enlightenment process may be the awareness that one is in need of psychological or psychiatric help.

humility in combination with the gifts of the Spirit, one is able to see oneself the way one truly is. Let us again remember that humility is just another word for self-knowledge. Hence, guided by these gifts a person is able to reflect upon his or her actions and is able to make powerful examinations of conscience which enable that person to see what he or she could not see before.

The gifts and virtues also enable a person to reach out to others, particularly spiritual friends, who will in authentic love tell that person what that person may not want to hear regarding his or her character. True love can be hurtful at first, but in the end, it is most precious. True love tells one what one needs to hear, not what one wants to hear!

Prayer in the Purgative Stage

Prayer in this initial stage of spirituality is primarily focused on prayers of petition. A person is still very much self-absorbed and thus such a person is primarily concerned with getting "goodies" from God, as opposed to loving God for simply being God.

When praying for others there is often a secondary motive for the prayer which has an intended beneficial benefit for the petitioner. For example, a brother may pray for another brother going through a difficult time, with the intention that God will bring relief; however, mixed within this petition will often be the hope that God will take care of this brother during this difficult time because one is tired of having to be concerned for the brother and one is tired of having to support the brother. One can see that the prayer is not completely pure. It has a secondary motive.

Charismatic prayer is a very popular form of prayer in this early stage of spiritual development. Charismatic prayer, as emphasized in today's society, is that form of prayer that is marked with the charisms of the Holy Spirit—in particular the ability to speak in tongues, to interpret tongues, to prophecy, and to experience being "slain in the Spirit" (cf. 1 Cor. 12:8-10). Charismatic prayer is most often associated with those in the purgative stage of spirituality since those in this stage tend to be intensely sense-oriented in their experiences of God. Hence, by its very nature, charismatic prayer is bound to give way to higher forms of prayer along the spiritual path. As one progresses in the spiritual life, God does more of the communicating, and individuals do more of the listening. As one progresses there is less noise and more silence. Charismatic prayer, as one progresses, becomes more insight and discernment-oriented.

Prayer in the purgative stage--in the early stages of development--is quite simplistic and filled with many distractions. John Cassian, who would eventually progress to be a saint, described this early stage of spirituality in his life:

> In my soul are countless and varied distractions. I am in a fever as my heart moves this way and that. I have no strength to hold in check the scatterings of my thoughts. I cannot utter my prayer without interruption, without being visited by empty images and by the memory of words and doings....[125]

Prayer is often filled with distractions and dryness at this stage because there is a battle going on. There is a battle going on between the anxieties of the world and the peace of Christ. There is a battle going on between self-will and God's will. The *Dark Nights* will be the purifying fires that will cleanse these aspects of the spiritual person (The *dark nights* will be discussed in the upcoming chapters). In many ways, a person in this stage is divided: He or she is a self-infatuated person while at the same time a struggling Christ-centered person. The battle between these two aspects of the person's life is painful and purging.

Dryness and Distractions

Dryness in prayer is something that needs to be particularly addressed at this stage as well as distractions. I will first deal with the dryness.

One of the most tragic circumstances in the spiritual life is that people of prayer stop praying when dryness enters into their prayer life. Dryness in prayer is associated with the loss of a sense of consolation, peace, happiness, comfort, and good feelings. Where once a person was enthusiastic in his or her prayer life, now the person loses this sense and begins to find prayer burdensome. Such people often remark: "I'm just too tired to pray tonight. I'll pray another time." In more tragic cases, people that experience dryness for the first time often abandon the spiritual life altogether—this is particularly true of neophytes who are unaware of what is going on in their souls.

Dryness is God's way of purifying prayer. It is easy to pray when one gets "goodies" from God, but God in the dryness of prayer is saying: "I now want you to pray to me out of pure faith. I want you to pray to me for simply being me, not for the "goodies" you get from me." If one perseveres in prayer during this dryness, one will exit the dryness as a person of much more profound spiritual insight. One will experience a newness of life that is associated with progress in the spiritual life. One comes out of the dryness a better, more

---

[125] *John Cassian: Conferences*, trans. Colm Luibheid (Mahwah: Paulist Press, 1985), Conference 10.

powerful, spiritual person. However, the sad reality is that too many people fail to persevere through the dryness. They give up so easily.

Hence, so many people who fail to persevere end up regressing. They stop praying until life becomes very empty. They restart their prayer life and find consolation and all the "goodies" associated with it. But then dryness again begins, and they again abandon prayer, until they feel a need for it. Life for such people is a continual cycle of progress and regression in the spiritual life. They move a little and then fall back again. They live their lives in this unending cycle, this unending cycle which hinders any great sense of fulfillment, peace, contentment, or happiness.

Life is filled with anxieties for such people for they fail to progress. That is why most Christians live and die in the purgative stage, for they fail to persevere in the battle of prayer. They are too willing to fall back on what they perceive as more safe. They fail to trust God enough. They fail to surrender to his will. They fail to realize that God knows what is best for our salvation and for our happiness. They fail to realize that he is the way, the truth, and the life (cf. Jn. 14:6).

Distraction is another factor that hinders most Christians in the spiritual life.   Distractions are brought about by a failure to surrender and trust completely in God. Consequently, life's problems and anxieties enter into the prayer life of the person. Distractions will slowly be calmed as one progresses in perseverance in the spiritual life of prayer.

One little technique that can often be used in moments of distractions is to have at hand a favorite word that reminds one of God (i.e., love, peace, hope, and so forth). Whenever the distractions enter into one's prayers, then one can call upon this word to help refocus one's prayer back on God.

Prayer is a spiritual battle. Let us fight the good fight (cf. 1 Tim. 6:12; 2 Tim. 4:7).

Beginning to See Christ in Others

While the purgative stage is primarily a self-centered stage, the grace of God is moving the person to see in others aspects of Christ, albeit at this stage the person only sees at a very superficial level. A person at this stage is able to see the Christ in the great saints, but has a great deal of trouble seeing the Christ in the neighbor. This stage is still a very self-absorbed stage in the spiritual journey.

Backsliding

A person in the purgative stage of the spiritual journey is always in danger of backsliding. This is particularly true when one enters the first *dark night*, which will be discussed in the next chapter. Thus, a person at this stage must hold unto the gift of faith as his or her guide.[126] One must hold unto the words of Jesus that remind the world that he came that all "may have life and have it abundantly" (Jn. 10:10), and one must hold unto the words of St. Paul that remind us that in Christ all "may be filled with the fullness of God" (Eph. 3:19).

The purgative stage of the spiritual journey is a painful one, yet it is not a stage that is without hope or direction. For the faithful one knows that by holding on, by fighting the good fight, by being courageous, by living one day at a time, and by surrendering more and more to God's will, victory and happiness are at hand. Serenity and peace are close by. One must find comfort in a prayer similar to that of Reinhold Niebuhr:

> God grant me the serenity to accept the things I cannot change, courage to change the things I can, and the wisdom to know the difference. Living one day at a time; enjoying one moment at a time; accepting hardships as the pathway to peace. Taking as Jesus did this sinful world as it is, not as I would have it; trusting that He will make all things right if I surrender to His will; that I may be reasonably happy in this life and supremely happy with Him forever in the next.

A person that fails to persevere will find himself or herself permanently trapped in the superficial purgative stage of spirituality, where no lasting authentic peace and contentment can be found, for by its nature this early stage is a painful, purging stage. Most Christians live and die in this purgative stage. That is why most Christians live and die as superficial Christians.

Failing to move forward is easy for the uncommitted, for it is always easier to go back to where one has been than to go forward into the unknown. The unknown can be frightening, and requires surrendering and trusting in God. Most people are afraid to surrender and to move into the sphere of the unknown, for God may ask them more than they are willing to give!

New vs. Old Self

In Christ one becomes a new creation (cf. 2 Cor. 5:17). The purgative stage is the beginning of this new creative, revolutionary process that is taking place in a person.

If one so chooses to move beyond this point and enter more profoundly into the unknown, into the mystery of God, then one will experience an ever more profound experience of life.

---

[126] Cf. *Ascent*, BK II, Ch. 4, nos. 2-3.

IV
The First Dark Night
The Active Purification of the Senses

> The greatest suffering of the souls in purgatory...is their awareness that something in them displeases God, that they have deliberately gone against His great goodness....[127]
>
> *St. Catherine of Genoa*

Purgatory will have to be done here on earth or in the afterlife, for heaven is a place of perfection. Let us seek to do our purgatory here on earth, for what greater gift of love can we give the Father?

The active purification of the senses is a time of purification of the senses that gives liberty to the Spirit. It is a time when a person "pommels [his or her] body and subdues it" (1 Cor. 9:27). It is a time when the person's inner being is being prepared for a state of existence where nature and grace complement each other, where the body does not cause any hindrance for the soul. It is a time when a re-directing of one's energies is taking place to fight off occasions of sins. It is a time when sensuality and irritability, which are the hallmarks of this stage of the spiritual journey, are curbed by a burning fire.[128] It is a time, as St. Maximus Confessor explains, when a person's "affective drive is wholly directed to God."[129]

This stage is called a *Dark Night* for it is a time when the senses are deprived of the consolations that are usually associated with a relationship with God. To the person who first enters this stage, the person may feel he or she is falling away from God, but in reality, he or she is closer to God than ever before in his or her spiritual journey. God is now asking the person to follow him in faith and not out of an infatuation or desire for consolations or "goodies" from God.

The active purification of the senses is a time when a person actively seeks to purify his or her being of those things that hinder the spiritual life and ultimately happiness. While grace is clearly present in the process most of the work being done in the purification process is being done by the individual who

---

[127] *Catherine of Genoa: Purgation and Purgatory*, trans. Serge Hughs (Mahwah: Paulist Press, 1979), 77f.

[128] Cf. IIa IIae, q. 35, a.1, ad 4um.

[129] *Maximus Confessor: Selected Writings*, trans. George C. Berthold (Mahwah: Paulist Press, 1985), Third Century, n. 98.

actively struggles to purify that which is contrary to the glory and honor of God In this active purification, the imagination, memory, intellect, and will begin to be purified of things that hinder a full experience of God. As William of St Thierry states:

> Man's part is continually to prepare his heart by ridding his will of foreign attachments, his reason or intellect of anxieties, his memory of idle or absorbing, sometimes even of necessary business, so that in the Lord's good time and when he sees fit, at the sound of the Holy Spirit's breathing, the elements which constitute thought may be free at once to come together and do their work, each contributing its share to the outcome of joy for the soul. The will displays pure affection for the joy which the Lord gives, the memory yields faithful material, the intellect affords the sweetness of experience....[130]

Imagination

A person cannot think without images in this early stage. An image always accompanies an idea. In the active purification of the imagination, the imagination is directed by reason illumined by faith. When the imagination is filled with impurities, the intellect is disrupted and damaged from functioning properly. If the imagination is cleansed from impurities, the imagination compliments the intellect in its proper functioning.[131] The imagination is a faculty of great power in the spiritual journey. It is in need of constant purifying, even in the highly advanced in the spiritual life.[132]

Memory[133]

Concupiscence and personal sin cause us to retain dangerous memories memories that hinder and stunt growth. As St. Maximus Confessor states, "the battle against memories is more difficult than the battle against deeds, as sinning in thought is easier than sinning in deed."[134]An ordered, healthy memory remembers the things of God, and a disordered memory forgets the good that God has done. For example, an individual who remembers the

---

[130] *William of St. Thierry: The Golden Epistle*, trans. Theodore Berkeley, OCSO (Kalamazoo: Cistercian Publications, Inc., 1971), n. 251.

[131] Cf. Ia, q. 78, a.4; q. 84, a.7.

[132] *Interior Castle*, 5th mansion, Ch. 4; 6th mansion, Ch. 1.

[133] *Ascent*, BK III, Chs. 1-15.

[134] *Maximus Confessor: Selected Writings*, trans. George C. Berthold (Mahwah: Paulist Press, 1985), First Century, n. 63.

wrongs that another person or persons has done to him or her, can at times have trouble forgiving that person or persons. The pain of the memory can preoccupy one with hatred and miserable feelings, and therefore hinder one's focus on God.

Such people are often prone to forgetting God (Cf. Jer. 2:32; Ps. 105:13, 21). Such a person is prone to being focused on the here and now as opposed to eternity. One needs to heal and order the memory to its proper functioning. The theological virtue of hope helps to heal the memory by helping the person avoid focusing on useless and dangerous memories. One's mind, directed by hope, turns to God.[135]

Intellect

The intellect can be wounded by concupiscence and personal sin. The wounded intellect leads to ignorance. It is wounded from perceiving truth and from grasping higher realities. One becomes absorbed in earthly considerations. One whose intellect is wounded is subject to neglect things of God and of salvation. One is prone to intellectual and spiritual pride and sloth, indifference, rash judgments, and spiritual and intellectual blindness. A person whose intellect is wounded is a person not willing to consult others, and not willing to listen to opposing opinions. Such a person thinks he or she knows it all (Mt. 23:16; 23f).[136]

The infused virtue of faith is the cure for a wounded intellect.[137] Faith is superior to reason and the senses. It enlightens reason, makes one adhere to truths and helps us judge according to these truths. Faith seeks understanding and the understanding that flows from this faith in turn nourishes the fruitfulness of faith.[138]

Will

The will is the faculty that tends toward the good known through the intellect. It has for its object the universal good that permits it to rise to the love of God. The will makes use of the other faculties, especially the intellect and the imagination, in guiding the person to the good.[139]

Concupiscence and personal sin cause defects in the will. Self-centeredness and egoism are the greatest wounds to the will. They lead one to forget the love of God and neighbor. They lead to thoughtlessness, agitation,

---

[135] *Ascent*, BK II, Chs. 10, 11, 16, 22; BK III, Chs. 6f and 14.
[136] Ia IIae, q. 85, a.3; IIa IIae, q. 15; q. 35, a.4, ad 3um; q. 138; q. 167, a.1.
[137] IIae IIae, q. 7, a.2; *Ascent*, BK III, 6f.
[138] *Ascent*, BK II, Ch. 3, 9, 11.
[139] Cf. Ia, q. 80, a.1f

discouragement, dissension, trouble, and anxiety. They lead to a battle where one tries to control God. They make one flee from all that requires sacrifice.

The cure for these wounds is found in the infused virtue of love.[140] Love moves one from being self-centered and ego-centered to other-centered. One becomes, through authentic love, a person for others.

> Take, Lord, and receive all my liberty, my memory, my understanding, and my entire will, all that I have and possess. You have given all to me; to you, O Lord, now I return it; all is yours, dispose of me wholly according to your Will. Give me only your love and your grace, for this is enough for me.

---

[140] *Ascent*, BK II, 6f.

V
The Second Part of the First Dark Night
The Passive Purification of the Senses

Lead, Kindly Light, amid the encircling gloom
Lead Thou me on!
The Night is dark, and I am far from home—
Lead Thou me on!
Keep Thou my feet; I do not ask to see
The distant scene—one step enough for me.

I was not ever thus, nor pray'd that Thou
Shouldst lead me on.
I loved to choose and see my path, but now
Lead Thou me on.
I loved the garish day, and, spite of fears,
Pride ruled my will: remember not past years.

So long Thy power hath blest me, sure it still
Will lead me on,
O'er moor and fen, o'er crag and torrent, till
The night is gone;
And with the morn those angel faces smile
Which I have loved long since, and lost awhile.[141]
John Henry Newman

In the active purification of the senses, the person did most of the work in response to grace in purifying the senses of all that was not for the honor and glory of God. Now in the passive purification, God is doing most of the work.[142]

In the passive purification of the senses, one moves from an imperfect stage in one's relationship with God, one where self-interest and self-satisfaction are the main emphasis, to a more perfect stage, where one's main emphasis is starting to be God-centered. One's emphasis is on, "What can I do for God?" as opposed to "What can God do for me?"[143]

The signs of this stage are well described by St. John of the Cross:[144]

---

[141] John Henry Newman, *Verses on Various Occasions* (London: Longmans, Green, and Co., 1910), 156-157.
[142] *Dark Night*, BK 1, Ch. 3.
[143] Cf. St. Catherine of Siena, *Dialogue*, Chs. 75, 144, 149.
[144] *Dark Night*, BK 1, Ch. 9; *Ascent*, BK II, Chs. 13f.

1) One finds no comfort in the things of God or in the things of the world. One's focus is no longer on the desires of the senses for their own sake. It is a time when one must will his or her being through this period of dryness.

2) Anxiety is symptomatic of this period of purification. One feels a sense that one is not serving God. In fact, one even senses that one is going backwards in the spiritual journey. One can become sluggish, weak, and even depressed in one's journey. Yet the desire, the will, continues to move one forward in serving God.

3) An inability to meditate, to reflect, and to excite the imagination are the hallmarks of this stage. God is beginning to be primarily experienced by means of the spirit as opposed to that of the senses.

It is crucially important to recognize that *all three* conditions must exist in the person at the *same time*; otherwise, what one is dealing with most likely is the result of a sinful life or a life wounded by a medical or psychological problem.

Initial Infused Contemplation

When the mind receives the representations of things, it of course patterns itself after each representation. In contemplating them spiritually it is variously conformed to each object contemplated. But when it comes to be in God, it becomes wholly without form and pattern, for in contemplating the one who is simple it becomes simple and entirely patterned in light.[145]

God at this stage is transforming meditation into a higher form of prayer initial infused contemplation. Contemplation transfers to the core of the person in a more profound manner the goods and energies which once were solely attained through the senses. Furthermore, it transfers to the core of the person spiritual gifts and strengths that transcend the ability of the internal and external senses to experience, because by its very nature contemplation is beyond the limits of the imagination and the gift of natural reason. It is because the gift of contemplation transcends the limits of the imagination and the gift of reason that the senses experience a sense of dryness, a sense of void. The reality is, however, that God is closest to the person at this stage for

---

[145] *Maximus Confessor: Selected Writings*, Third Century, n. 97.

he is asking the person to love him in pure faith as opposed to loving him for the good things he gives.

In this initial stage of contemplation, a person is not yet completely aware of what is going on. All that one is aware of is that there is an inner desire for solitude and quiet.

While one has begun to enter into the initial sphere of contemplation at this stage of the spiritual life, one has not completely become removed from the ability of discursive meditation. In fact, at this stage, it is not unusual for a person to move back and forth between meditation and contemplation. When meditation is fruitful, then one should remain at this stage of prayer until God moves one forward. If meditation becomes dry, then one is being moved in grace to contemplation.[146]

Contemplation is fruitful when it becomes less and less distracted by concepts or thoughts. When one becomes overly burdened by these distractions, God is calling one back to the state of meditation. When one feels an inability to meditate, to use concepts and thoughts in prayer, then one is being called to contemplation.[147]

The Jesus Prayer

The *Jesus prayer* is often helpful during this transition from meditation to initial infused contemplation. The *Jesus prayer* is the unceasing repetition of the phrase "Lord Jesus Christ, Son of God, have mercy on me a sinner." One seeks during this repetition to find a state where one gazes at the heart of God without images or idle thoughts.[148]

Centering Prayer/Technique

Centering prayer is a powerful gift at this stage of the spiritual life. St. Teresa of Avila alludes to this reality in chapter 31,7 of her book *The Way of Perfection*. Centering prayer is a technique whereby a person chooses a favorite word, "a gentle word" (or even an image) that reminds him or her of God and then uses this word or image to chase away distractions to contemplative prayer. At this initial stage of infused contemplation, distractions are normal; hence, a centering word or image can help--in grace-- move a person into a deeper experience of contemplation.

---

[146] Cf. *Dark Night*, BK 1, Ch. 10; *Ascent*, BK II, Ch. 13; *Life*, Ch. 14.
[147] Cf. Evargrius Ponticus, *The 153 Chapters on Prayer*, 9, 44, 69-70, 120.
[148] See John Climacus: *The Ladder of Divine Ascent*, trans. Colm Luibheid (Mahwah: Paulist Press, 1982), 103, 239, 262, 266, 274-276, 278-279, 286, 290.

Gifts of the Spirit
The gifts of the Spirit are flowering at this point, particularly the gifts of knowledge, understanding, fortitude, and the fear of the Lord.

Knowledge
One begins to know the fact that the things of the world are empty unless they are directed to the glory and honor of God.[149]

Understanding
One begins to penetrate the deeper aspects of the faith. One is cleansing one's experience of the faith of all phantasms, misrepresentations, and errors. One is moving beyond simple adherence to formulas and the simple recitation of prayers, to a more penetrating experience of those formulas and recited prayers.[150]

Fortitude
The desire to serve God at all cost is beginning to take effect. One is willing to follow in Christ's footsteps and carry the cross. The virtues of patience and longanimity are enhanced by this gift as one manages the trials and tribulations of life with Christ-like courage.[151]

Fear of the Lord
This gift of the Spirit makes one fear sin. "My flesh trembles for fear of thee, and I am afraid of thy judgments" (Ps. 118:120). This gift profoundly strengthens the person to live a virtuous, patient and chaste life out of fear of being condemned to hell.[152] Sins against chastity and patience are the hallmark of this level of the spiritual life.[153] When one enters into the deeper stages of the spiritual life, the fear of hell will be replaced by the fear of not loving enough.

How to get out of the Dark Night
St. John of the Cross teaches his disciples how one is to progress through the *dark night*:[154]

    1)   One must have an enlightened spiritual director.

---

[149] IIa IIae, q. 9, a.4.
[150] IIa IIae, q. 8, a.7; q. 61, a.5.
[151] Cf. IIa IIae, q. 139, a.2.
[152] Cf. IIa IIae, q. 19, a. 9, a. 19.
[153] *Dark Night*, BK 1, Ch. 14.
[154] Ibid., Ch. 10.

2) One must persevere in patience, trust, and humility through this difficult time.
3) One must keep one's being focused on Jesus and his cross.
4) One must foster a docile spirit where one is open to God's providence.
5) One must will oneself through this period of purification in faith.

The Effects of the Passive Purification of the Senses

The passive purification of the senses has subjected the senses to the Spirit. Our senses have been spiritualized. One is moved more by an attraction to God for being God as opposed to God for being a giver of things. One begins to have a profound knowledge of God and self. One becomes aware of a new sense of power in fighting sin and in penetrating the mysteries of God. The person is beginning to see the world and one's being as never before. One is entering the sphere of enlightenment.[155] One is entering the sphere of dependence on God and a joyful surrendering to God's will.

An Aside

The Dark Night and Psychological Considerations

The *dark night* of the senses and the *dark night* of the soul (which will be discussed just before the unitive stage) can be very confusing to people who are experiencing them and who are observing them. This is a very delicate and crucial time in the spiritual journey. Great harm can be done by spiritual directors, psychologists, and psychiatrists if they are not aware of what is going on. The sad reality of today is that most priests are inadequately trained in the field of spirituality and in the field of psychology or psychiatry, and the same can be said of psychologists and psychiatrists: most lack an understanding of spiritual theology. Hence, great harm can be caused to the person's spiritual journey, either by retarding their progress or leaving them in a stupor of uncertainty and confusion, when improper advice is given. It is of great relief that the Roman schools of theology have greatly emphasized this interaction between the psychological and the spiritual. It is my hope that this will filter down to all seminaries in the training of priests.

Given what has been said, it is unrealistic for a priest to have adequate training in the field of psychology or psychiatry, given that the most basic training of priests takes nine to ten years. Likewise, it is unrealistic for psychologist and psychiatrists to have an adequate training in spiritual theology, given their own extensive years of studies. The solution is to seek out a cooperative interaction in the counseling of persons. As the cliché goes: Two

---

[155] Cf. Ibid., Chs. 12 and 13; Siena, *Dialogue*, Ch. 4; *Life*, Ch. 31.

minds are better than one. A person can rightly claim, therefore, that two or three fields of study are better than one.

What is the harm that can be done by the misdiagnosis of a person? The danger for the uninformed spiritual director is that what may very well be a pathological condition in need of either psychological counseling or psychiatric help in the form of medication, or both, can be left untreated. The person in such a case may in fact not be experiencing a *dark night* at all. They may indeed simply be experiencing a psychological breakdown or the development of a "chemical imbalance." Failure to bring this to the attention of a psychologist or psychiatrist can be extremely harmful to the person. On the other hand, if a person is experiencing an authentic *dark night* then the use of medication can be extremely harmful to the progress of the person, for the medication could very well eliminate the very function of the *dark night*, the purification of the person's being.

Purification is by its very nature a painful experience--to medicate the painful experience so that one experiences bliss will only retard the very purpose of the *dark night*. It will definitely stifle the purgative process and can in fact lead one to regress back to a lower form of the spiritual life.

A final point to be made is that at times, one may find a person authentically experiencing a *dark night* and also experiencing a pathological disorder. This is a case where the close interaction of the spiritual director and the psychologist or psychiatrist is essential. Having said all this, the following is a brief guideline in helping one understand what is authentically a part of the *dark night* and what is more of a psychological or pathological problem.

Faith, hope, and love are the distinguishing marks between the *dark nights* and patently pathological conditions.

In the *dark nights*, no matter how bad things get, even to the edge of despair, there is always a sense of faith and hope, a sense that one will be able to will one's very self through the situation in grace. There is a sense of trust that God is in control and that even though a person may not be clear as to where God is taking him or her, there is the clear understanding that God will not leave the person abandoned. The will and trust—empowered by grace--to move on is never extinguished no matter how bad things get. Furthermore, and more importantly, one never loses a sense of the love of God or of neighbor in the *dark nights*. No matter how wrenching the pain of the purgation, the love of God remains and the love of neighbor remains. The striving for being a person for others always remains. Humility, patience, and calm grow during these *dark nights*—particularly when the individual is in the hands of a competent spiritual director.

In a pathological situation, the faith of a person is deeply damaged and can be lost at an explicit level. The ability to will one's being through the situation is often impossible. Trust is often lost. The future looks bleak. There is seemingly no hope, without a drastic change. Love of neighbor is often replaced by a dislike or hate for others. One becomes excessively or obsessively introspective or self-absorbed to the point of losing sight of concerns for others. Love of God is often turned into a sense of indifference or even bitter anger toward him. The sense that one is being purged is often replaced with the sense that one is cursed. One can begin to lose a grip on reality.

These key factors, when explored by competent individuals in the fields of spirituality, psychology, and psychiatry, are of great importance in determining whether one is experiencing a *dark night* or whether one is experiencing a pathological disturbance

The ultimate sign that one has gone through the *dark night* is that one comes out of it renewed and prepared for a deeper prayer and spiritual life. The ultimate sign that one has not gone through a *dark night* is that one becomes increasingly ill, with no cure in sight, until one turns to professional help.

VI
The Illuminative Stage
A Time of Enlightenment

Again Jesus spoke to them, saying, "I am the light of the world; he who follows me will not walk in darkness, but will have the light of life" (Jn. 8:12).

In the purgative stage the individual grows to love God with his or her whole heart primarily by means of the faculties of the senses. In the illuminative stage one begins to love God not only with one's whole heart, but also with one's whole soul. This love transcends the limits of the senses. In the final stage, the unitive stage of the spiritual journey, love becomes complete. One at this stage loves God with one's whole heart, soul, strength, and mind.

In the illuminative stage, the ease of prayer returns after the darkness. A greater capacity for work, service, teaching, directing, and organizing takes place at this stage. The illuminative stage is exemplified by "good works." It is the beginning of the mystical life. It is the time when everyday mysticism is experienced. As Karl Rahner states, it is a stage in life

--where one dares to pray into silent darkness and knows that one is heard, although no answer seems to come back about which one might argue and rationalize,
--where one lets oneself go unconditionally and experiences this capitulation as true victory,
--where falling becomes true uprightness,
--where desperation is accepted and is still secretly accepted as trustworthy without cheap trust,
--where a man entrusts all his knowledge and all his questions to the silent and all-inclusive mystery which is loved more than all our individual knowledge which makes us such small people,
--where we rehearse our death in everyday life and try to live in such a way as we would like to die, peaceful and composed....[156]

This is the mystical walk with and in God. This is the "mysticism of everyday life."

---

[156] Karl Rahner, *The Spirit in the Church*, trans. John Griffiths (New York: The Seabury Press, 1979), 21-22.

In the illuminative stage, the acquired virtues that were primaril' predominant in the purgative stage are now brought to the service of th infused virtues. The acquired virtues and the infused virtues, therefore, wor hand in hand for the good of the person's growth in the life of God.[157]

The virtues come together like never before in the illuminative stage. Th' acquired virtue of prudence and the infused virtue of prudence work hand an' hand and are aided by the Spirit's gift of counsel. The fruits of this interactio' are foresight, circumspection, and constancy. The acquired virtue of fortitud' and the infused virtue of fortitude work hand and hand and are aided by th' Spirit's gift of fortitude. The fruits of this interaction are patience magnanimity, and longanimity. The acquired virtue of justice and the infuse' virtue of justice work hand and hand and are aided by the Spirit's gift of piet' The fruits of this interaction are obedience and a call for penance and religior The acquired virtue of temperance and the infused virtue of temperance wor hand and hand and are aided by the Spirit's gift of fear. The fruits of thi interaction are chastity, meekness, and poverty.[158]

Acquired Prudence (cf. Prov. 14:15; 1 Pet. 4:7)

> The mind that has succeeded in the active life advances in prudence....[159]

Acquired prudence is that moral virtue that directs through right reaso acts of justice, courage, temperance, and their related virtues. It preserves a individual from impulsiveness in temperament, imagination, and sensibl appetites. It moves one to seek advice, obey what is reasonable, and gives th strength to deal with differences in the temperament of different character At this stage of the spiritual journey, the acquired virtue of prudence is we developed and prepares one for the powerful response to the infused gift c prudence—that moral virtue that is grace-elevated.[160]

Infused Prudence

Infused prudence is that moral virtue that transcends the limits of th natural gift of right reason. It is in a sense the consequence of taking a acquired moral virtue and infusing it with grace. Grace elevates that which wa natural into the realm of that which is supernatural. The infused moral virtu

---

[157] Cf. Ia IIae, q. 63, a.4.
[158] Cf. Ia IIae, q. 63, a.4.
[159] *Maximus Confessor: Selected Writings*, Second Century, n. 26.
[160] Cf. Ia IIae, q. 58, a.5; q. 64, a.1.

of prudence is given in response to grace. It is marked by a profound love and zeal for God and for the burning desire for the salvation and good of all people. It directs all the virtues to that which can be considered their last end, which is God's eternal destiny for all. All acts are judged according to a pilgrim's eternal destiny. The focus is on eternity, and not simply on the temporal aspects of life, which the acquired virtues tend to be primarily focused on.[161]

The gift of counsel accompanies the infused moral virtue of prudence. Wise decisions are made which are based on the knowledge of self and God. This leads to mercy, the beatitude of mercy, for a person with the infused moral virtue of prudence is able to find a comfortable milieu between rigor and justice. It also leads to the preferential option for mercy.[162]

Foresight, circumspection, and constancy are the quintessential marks of a person with prudence in the illuminative stage of the spiritual journey. One is blessed with an elevated sense of foresight and circumspection; that is, that grace-empowered ability to consider all circumstances and their possible consequences, particularly as they pertain to one's eternal destiny. One is also blessed with the gift of constancy, that ability to remain--as a consequence of the insights brought about through foresight and circumspection--steadfast in faith in whatever life may bring.[163]

Prudence and Simplicity

Prudence moves a person to live life simply. Prudence enables an individual to do the most little of things in the most holy of manners.[164] St. Therese of Lesieux's *little way* exemplifies this reality.

Acquired and Infused Fortitude

The acquired moral virtue of courage or fortitude is elevated by grace into the realm of infused courage or fortitude. Aided by the Spirit's gift of fortitude, the moral virtue of fortitude raises an individual to new heights in the spiritual life, to new heights in patience, magnanimity, and longanimity or forbearance.

A person experiencing the grace of fortitude is a person whose patience in times of difficulty does not allow him or her to depart from right reason illumined by faith. Such a person has the patience and forbearance to endure and fight off any temptations that might cause him or her to yield to difficulties. One at this stage is able to bear, often beyond the natural abilities

---

[161] Cf. Ia, q. 79, a.9.
[162] Cf. IIa IIae, q. 52, a.4.
[163] Cf. Ia IIa, q. 63, a.4.
[164] Cf. IIa IIae, q. 109, a.2 ad 4um.

of the body, adversity, sadness, and injuries of all sorts for whatever length of time.

Such a person is able to see and bear the cross. This seeing and bearing of the cross is done with magnanimity, with a sense of calm and sacrifice. The end of the difficulty is seen, the victory of the cross is clearly perceived in such a person. Because of this reality, such an individual experiences a loftiness of spirit enabling him or her to disdain any hint of meanness or revenge as a consequence of the adversity encountered.[165]

Acquired and Infused Justice

Justice is a movement away from self-infatuation and a movement toward the good of others (cf. Lev. 19:15; Col. 4:1). Again, as with all the moral virtues, the acquired moral virtue of justice is at the service of the infused, grace-filled moral virtue of justice. Aided by the Spirit's gift of piety, a person exemplifies a life of authentic faith and works.[166]

When discussing the moral virtue of justice, one must take into account the three expressions of justice that a person at this stage of the spiritual journey is radically aware of.

1. *Commutative Justice*: Commutative justice is aimed at the dignity of equality. Because of this reality, it is a form of justice that fights against any occurrences of theft, fraud, usury, false accusations, insults, unjust blame, defamation, slander, gossip, insinuation, and so on.[167]

2. *Distributive Justice*: Distributive justice is aimed at how public goods are used. It fights against any hint of favoritism, oppression, unrelieved poverty, and corruption of all kinds.[168]

3. *Social Justice*: Social justice or legal justice is preoccupied with the common good of society. It demands personal sacrifice,[169] and is inseparable from prayer:

> Action and contemplation now grow together into one life and one unity. They become two aspects of the same thing. Action is charity looking outward to other men, and contemplation is charity drawn inward to its own divine source. Action is the stream, and contemplation is the spring. The spring remains more important

---

[165] Cf. IIa IIae, q. 136, a.1.
[166] Cf. Ia IIae, q. 56, a.6, c and ad 3um.
[167] Cf. IIa IIae, q. 73-75.
[168] Cf. IIa IIae, q. 63, a.1f.
[169] Cf. IIa IIae, q. 58, a.6f.

than the stream, for the only thing that really matters is for love to spring up inexhaustibly from the infinite abyss of Christ and of God.[170]

Guiding all three of these expressions of justice is that gift of *epikeia*, that gift that preserves the dignity of the human person at all cost, that gift that recognizes the spirit as well as the letter of the law.[171]

Justice and Veracity

Justice and veracity are intertwined with prudence and simplicity. Justice and veracity however are predominantly concerned with moral integrity, with telling the truth and acting according to it. In the illuminative stage sins of duplicity, hypocrisy, boasting, and mockery are extinguished.[172] There are no two-faced saints!

Acquired and Infused Temperance

Temperance elevated by grace to what is referred to as infused temperance--and aided by the Spirit's gift of fear--is that moral virtue that is exemplified by a sense of moderation in thought, action and feeling (cf. Sir. 5:2; 18:30; 37:27-31; Titus 2:12). Temperance finds its most precious expression in the evangelical counsels[173] of poverty, chastity, and obedience. Meekness (that ability to endure persecutions or injustices with patience and without resentment) is also a significant expression at this stage of the spiritual journey.

The Evangelical Counsels

Poverty is that gift that purifies a person of all attachments. It is that gift that unites the person to Christ Jesus. For St. Thomas Aquinas, Christ chose a life of poverty for four reasons, four reasons that all disciples are all called to imitate.[174]

1. Poverty frees one from the cares that are associated with earthly goods.
2. Poverty frees one to be concerned with the salvation of souls.
3. Poverty frees one for the desire of eternal goods.

---

[170] Merton, *No Man is an Island* (New York: Image Books, 1967), 65.

[171] Cf. IIa IIae, q. 120, a.1f

[172] Cf. IIa IIae, q. 109, a.2 ad 4um.

[173] The evangelical counsels are responsible for the majority of the grace-filled work of detachment that is necessary for holiness and thus happiness.

[174] III a, q. 40, a.3; q. 35, a.7.

4. Poverty frees one, in the absence and contradiction of earthly helps, to express the divine power that saves souls.

Poverty is true freedom. It moves the clouds of worldly attachments away from the spiritual life and detaches one of all that is not for the glory and honor of God. Love of God, love of neighbor and love of heaven are the all-consuming hungers of the poor in spirit.[175]

Chastity of heart and body are exemplified in the infused moral virtue of temperance. Whether one is a virgin, a religious, or a single, unmarried person, all are called to a chaste life, a life free of lewdness or salaciousness, a life which is pure in thought and action. It is empowered by the grace that accompanies the love of neighbor and the love of God.[176]

Obedience is a joyful submissiveness to that which is best for one's eternal salvation. Obedience delivers a person away from the slavery that is attached to self-will and self-infatuation. The fruits of obedience, thus, are rectitude, or righteousness in judgment, which is accompanied by a liberty of spirit: "Now the Lord is the Spirit, and where the Spirit of the Lord is, there is freedom" (2 Cor. 3:17).

Theological Virtues of Faith Hope and Love
Faith

Faith is a gift (Eph. 2:8) aided by the gift of understanding which is in conformity with reason, yet transcends the limits of reason.[177] Faith in the illuminative stage is freed to a great extent of all aspects of egoism, passions, jealousies, whims, etc., of all that can damage a person's response to the inner call of grace. For some at this stage, faith is greater in the faculty of the intellect, thereby producing the fruits of certitude and firmness in actions. In others, faith is greater in the will, thereby producing the fruits of devotion and confidence.[178] In either case, all aspects of one's life are being guided by the light of faith, which guides the individual to his or her eternal destiny of loving God for being God (Rom. 8:28).

Hope

Hope is that confidence in the help of God. Hope helps one to persevere (Mt. 10:22) and overcome trials and tribulations (Rom. 5:2-5). Hope, because of these trials and tribulations, purifies the person for the love of God (Cf. Wis

---

[175] Cf. IIa, q. 23, a.1, ad 3um.
[176] Cf. IIa IIae, q. 151, a. 1-3.
[177] Cf. IIa IIae, q. 15.
[178] IIa IIae, q. 5, a.4.

3: 4-6). Hope is a walk into the mystery of the unknown. Yet it is a walk with a certain sense of certitude of direction. Hope makes a person advance more generously toward God by giving the person a greater desire for him. God becomes a person's end; God becomes all that is hoped for.

In the illuminative stage two lingering defects from the purgative stage are being polished off: *presumption and discouragement*. Presumption is that defect that fails to recognize the necessity of responding to grace in the spiritual journey. It is that defect that overemphasizes God's mercy and underemphasizes God's justice. Hence, people often feel they can be pardoned without repentance or in the worst case they can even feel assured of salvation. In the case of the defect of discouragement at this stage, a person can often feel that the spiritual journey is too difficult and thus hopeless. One often turns away from grace and goes back to a former way of life because one senses that grace is too inaccessible. In the illuminative stage these two defects against hope, against properly ordered confidence in God, are being completely finished off, completely extinguished.

Love

For John Climacus, "Love, by its nature, is a resemblance to God."[179] Love is the conformity of a person's will to God's, for all the other virtues follow the virtue of love (cf. 1 Cor. 13:4). In the illuminative stage, certain signs can be seen according to St. Thomas Aquinas:[180]

1. Mortal sins are a thing of the past, since love has conquered that inclination.
2. Because of love, earthly things such as pleasures, honors, wealth, etc., are no longer of great interest.
3. Because of love, one seeks to be engulfed in the presence of God, to love him, to think of him, to adore him, to pray to him, to thank him, to ask his pardon, to aspire to him.
4. One desires, out of the grace of love, to please God more than anything and anyone in the entire created realm of reality.
5. One seeks to love and know God in one's neighbor, in spite of the neighbor's defects. One loves one's neighbor for simply being a child of God, a child of God who is beloved by God. One loves in the illuminative stage God in one's neighbor and one's neighbor in God. Love of God and love of neighbor merge into one reality.

---

[179] *John Climacus: The Ladder of Divine Ascent*, Step. 30, 286.
[180] Ia IIae, q. 112, a.5.

75

In the words of Dorothy Day, "we cannot love God unless we love each other, and to love we must know each other."[181] Love of neighbor is the most distinguishing characteristic of the illuminative stage (Cf. Mt. 5:44, 47, 48).

Zeal

> Dearest Lord, teach me to be generous. Teach me to serve You as you deserve; to give and not to count the cost; to fight and not to heed the wounds; to toil and not to seek for rest; to labor and not to ask for reward, save that of knowing that I am doing Your will. Amen.

The illuminative stage of the spiritual journey is marked with tremendous zeal. It is a holy zeal that is directed toward the glory and honor of God and in particular the salvation of persons. Unlike the zeal that is predominant in the purgative stage, this zeal is not lost during times of trials and tribulations, nor is it susceptible to bitterness.

Motives for Zeal
Zeal is nourished by a deep grace-filled thirst to love God and neighbor above all. It is signified by the following marks:
1. An intense desire to imitate Christ in all things.
2. An intense desire to bring all people into the kingdom of God.
3. An intense desire to overcome the enemies of the Church.
4. An intense desire to overcome indifference, inertia, lack of comprehension, ill will, and spiteful opposition.

Qualities of Holy Zeal
Holy zeal is enlightened by the light of faith. It is the fruit of the acquired and infused moral virtues, particularly the virtue of prudence and the gifts of the Holy Spirit, particularly the gifts of wisdom and counsel. Unlike bitter zeal, which is not of God, and which is self-seeking, proud, insensitive, impatient, rude and hate-filled, holy zeal, which is of God, is calm, humble, meek, patient, sensitive, and always other-centered. This type of zeal is expressed in the traditional spiritual and corporal works of mercy:

Corporal Works of Mercy
- Feeding the hungry

---

[181] Day, *The Long Loneliness*, 317.

- Giving drink to the thirsty
- Clothing the naked
- Sheltering the homeless
- Visiting the sick
- Visiting the imprisoned

<u>Spiritual Works of Mercy</u>
- Instructing the ignorant
- Correcting sinners
- Advising the doubtful
- Showing patience to sinners and those in error
- Forgiving others
- Confronting the afflicted
- Praying for the living and the dead

In her fight against the injustices of the world, Dorothy Day could say with great ease: "It is natural for me to stand my ground...using...weapons as the works of mercy to show love and alleviate suffering."[182]

The Holy Spirit in the Illuminative Stage
Wisdom, the highest of the gifts of the Spirit, at this stage of the spiritual life is very active in directing all the other gifts in the grace-filled, zeal-driven, saint of God.[183]

Fear
The gift of fear supplies strength to overcome the imperfections that are often intertwined with the virtues. In the purgative stage, the gift of fear tends to be one that is more servile in nature; that is, a person grows in the spiritual life out of a fear of eternal damnation. In the illuminative stage, the gift of fear is transformed into what has been traditionally called filial fear; that is, a fear that empowers the spiritual life not so much out of a fear of hell as much as a fear of not loving enough. For the people at this stage, the big fear consists in having to face Jesus after their earthly journey without having loved enough.

Love for the poor becomes very powerful at this stage, and thus the gift of fear in the illuminative stage is tied to the beatitude of the love for the poor.[184]

---

[182] Day, *The Long Loneliness*, 206.
[183] Ia IIae, q. 68, a.7.
[184] Cf. IIa IIae, q. 19.

St. Vincent de Paul would say: "it is better to feed the poor than to raise the dead."

Piety

The gift of piety is the gift of rendering to God what is rightly due to God. Human reason becomes illumined by faith at this stage like never before. Suffering takes on meaning and a sense of sweetness.[185]   As John Henry Newman explains, "I am, I can never be thrown away. If I am in sickness, my sickness may serve Him; in perplexity, my perplexity may serve Him; if I am in sorrow, my sorrow may serve Him."[186] At this stage one finds in the mystery of suffering the mystery of love, and one finds in the mystery of love the mystery of suffering.

Prayer becomes more fervent and persistent as new insights into the mystery of life become illumined. Any hint of hardness of heart is replaced with an open heart. This predisposes a person to being open to interior silence, recollection, and detachment. The gift of piety corresponds, as a consequence, to the beatitude that emphasizes the power and preciousness of the meek.[187]

Knowledge

The gift of knowledge is a gift that elevates human knowledge to new heights. At this stage there is a radical knowledge of those things that are of God and those things that are not of God. The knowledge of good and evil is powerfully perceived and felt with great sorrow at this stage.   In the illuminative stage, the gift of knowledge is powerfully tied to the beatitude of the sorrowful.[188]

Fortitude

In the illuminative stage there is a heightened desire to fight the temptations of the flesh, the world, and the devil. There is also a heightened degree of patience and perseverance in the quest for justice. This stage is often associated with the beatitude regarding those who hunger and thirst for justice.[189]

---

[185] Cf. IIa IIae, q. 121.
[186] John Henry Newman, *Meditations and Devotions* (Westminster, MD: Christian Classics, 1975), 301.
[187] Cf. IIa IIae, q. 121.
[188] Cf. IIa IIae, q. 9.
[189] Cf. IIa IIae, q. 139, a.1, 2.

Counsel

This gift overcomes the imperfections that hinder the virtue of prudence. It corresponds to the beatitude of the merciful, in that all actions are decided in favor of authentic mercy, a mercy that is properly balanced with justice. The gift of counsel at this stage also helps avoid the dangers of temerity, of recklessness and rashness, which often lead to unhealthy and even evil fanaticism. On the other hand, the gift of counsel helps to fight the danger of pusillanimity--that is, cowardliness and timidity in the face of danger or opposition.[190]

Understanding

Understanding in the illuminative stage is enlightened by the interior light of grace. Its primary impact in this stage of a person's journey is in helping to eliminate the imperfections that hinder the deep penetrations into the truths of faith. The gift of understanding is primarily directed to the purification of one's intentions; thus, it is often viewed to correspond to the beatitude of the pure of heart.[191] This purity of heart and deep penetration into the faith can be seen in St. Hildegard of Bingen's reflection on the nature of the Trinity:

> [As] the flame of a fire has three qualities, so there is one God in three Persons. How? A flame is made up of a brilliant light and red power and fiery heat. It has brilliant light that it may shine, and red power that it may endure, and fiery heat that it may burn. Therefore, by the brilliant light understand the Father, Who with paternal love opens His brightness to His faithful; and by the red power, which is in the flame that it may be strong, understand the Son, Who took on a body born from a Virgin, in which His divine wonders are shown; and by the fiery heat understand the Holy Spirit, Who burns ardently in the minds of the faithful. But there is no flame seen where there is neither brilliant light nor red power nor fiery heat; and thus also where neither the Father nor the Son nor the Holy Spirit is known God is not properly worshipped.[192]

---

[190] Cf. IIa IIae, q. 139, a.1, 2.

[191] Cf. IIa IIae, q. 8, a.1, 4, 6, 7.

[192] *Hildegard of Bingen: Scivias*, trans. Mother Columba Hart and Jane Bishop (Mahwah: Paulist Press, 1990), BK II, Vision II, n. 6.

Eternal Wisdom shall be my bride, and I will be her Servitor. Oh God, if I could catch one glimpse of her, speak to her for a few moments.[193]

The highest of the gifts of the Spirit, wisdom, helps one judge all things in relation to God. Since all is seen in terms of God's providence and his will, then one in this stage of the spiritual journey experiences a sense of peace.[194] In the words of Dorothy Day,

I should know by this time that just because I feel that everything is useless and going to pieces and badly done and futile, it is not really that way at all. Everything is all right. It is in the hands of God. Let us abandon everything to Divine Providence.[195]

Wisdom brings about peace. One is in peace and one seeks to bring this peace to others. This gift corresponds, therefore, to the beatitude of the peacemakers.[196]

The Ten Commandments (Ex. 20:2-17; Dt. 5:26)[197]

Through the working of the commandments the mind puts off the passions.[198]
                                                    St. Maximus Confessor

1. I am the Lord your God: you shall not have strange gods before me.
2. You shall not take the name of the Lord your God in vain.
3. Remember to keep holy the Lord's Day.
4. Honor your father and your mother.
5. You shall not kill.
6. You shall not commit adultery.
7. You shall not steal.

---

[193] *Henry Suso's Life*, in *Exemplar: Life and Writings of Blessed Henry Suso* (Dubuque: Priory Press, 1962), vol. I, 3.
[194] Cf. IIa IIae, q. 45, a.1, 2, 5, 6.
[195] Dorothy Day, *House of Hospitality* (New York: Sheed and Ward, 1939), 101.
[196] Cf. IIa IIae, q. 45, a.1, 2, 5, 6.
[197] CCC 2084-2550.
[198] *Maximus Confessor: Selected Writings*, First Century, n. 94.

8. You shall not bear false witness against your neighbor.
9. You shall not covet your neighbor's wife.
10. You shall not covet your neighbor's goods.

1. The first commandment forbids acts of voluntary doubt (the disregarding or refusing to believe as true what God has revealed), incredulity (the refusal to assent to truth), heresy (the denial of truth), apostasy (the rejection of the Christian faith), schism (refusal to submit to the Catholic Church), despair (ceasing to hope in salvation), presumption (the counting on one's own capacities for salvation), indifference (the failure to appreciate or care in God's goodness), ingratitude (the refusal to return love for love), lukewarmness (a hesitation in responding to God's love), spiritual sloth (refusing the joy that comes from God), hatred of God (denying God's goodness), idolatry (divinizing worldly "things" such as power, pleasure, race, country, etc.), sacrilege (profaning things and persons of God), atheism (denial of God's existence), and agnosticism (a refusal to affirm or deny the existence of God). Occult beliefs and practices such as superstition, divination, magic and sorcery are also forbidden.

2. The second commandment demands a respect for the sacredness of the Lord's name. Acts of blasphemy (asserting words or thoughts of hatred, reproach, or defiance against God), the taking of oaths (the superficial misuse or lack of respect for God's name), false oaths (swearing to take God as a witness to something that is not true), and perjury (making a promise under oath with no intention of keeping it) are sinful.

3. The third commandment is a summons to keep the Lord's Day a holy day. It demands the faithful attendance of Sunday Mass, and an attitude of profound worship. It is a time to spend with God and to abstain from any work that distracts from authentically consecrating Sunday as a precious day of love of God and love of neighbor. One seeks comfort, but one also seeks to be challenged to grow.

4. The fourth commandment demands the authentic honoring of father and mother. Children owe just obedience, respect, gratitude, assistance, and the repaying of love for love to their parents. Parents have the responsibility of caring for their children's physical and spiritual needs, fostering a vocation, and teaching them to serve and

81

follow God above all. The family forms the foundation for societal and ecclesiastical life.

5. The fifth commandment is an affirmation of the dignity of life. Being created in the image and likeness of God, the human person is sacred from conception to natural death. Murder is a violation of the dignity of the person and the creator. Unjust war, direct abortions intentional euthanasia, abortion-causing contraceptives, and suicide are forbidden by this commandment.

6. The sixth commandment is a command that demands fidelity. Any act which is contrary to the dignity of chastity, such as fornication adultery, polygamy, divorce and remarriage (without an annulment) open or free marriages, same-sex marriages or unions, homosexual and bisexual acts, masturbation, contraceptive use, pornography prostitution, incest and rape are forbidden. Artificial insemination and the use of a surrogate uterus are forbidden. The sixth commandment is a call to authentic sexual integration, authentic life and love.

7. The seventh commandment is a prohibition against stealing. Stealing is characteristic of a lack of charity and injustice. Often stealing is done in subtle ways: For example, on the part of employers in a business a violation of the seventh commandment is often exemplified by business fraud, ignorance of contracts, and the mistreatment of workers through unfair wages and lack of health and retirement benefits. On the part of the employee this injustice and lack of charity is often seen in acts of laziness and all forms of lack of effort in the work environment. The seventh commandment forbids social relationships based solely on economic factors, as opposed to the nature of the human person. It acknowledges that the goods of creation are for the entire human family. The "author, center, and goal of all economic and social life is the human person." The seventh commandment demands the tithing of one's talent and treasure to God.

8. The eighth commandment is a prohibition against bearing false witness against one's neighbor. Lying, duplicity, hypocrisy, boasting dissimulation (hiding under a false appearance), rash judgment (assuming without reason the moral fault of another), detraction (disclosing another's faults to someone who did not know them),

82

betrayal of confidences, calumny (character assassination), and slander (a false statement that damages a person's reputation) are all acts contrary to the dignity of persons.

9. The ninth commandment is a prohibition against coveting one's neighbor's wife. It prohibits moral permissiveness, and seeks the purification of the social moral climate. This commandment calls one to live a life of decency, chastity and modesty. It is a call for purity of heart, intention, and vision.

10. The tenth commandment is a call to avoid coveting another's goods. It is a call to avoid greed, envy, and all immoderate desires. It is a call to desire a detachment from all that is contrary to the glory and honor of God. One is called to desire God above all.

Discernment of Spirits[199]

> Beware of false prophets, who come to you in sheep's clothing but inwardly are ravenous wolves (Mt. 7:15).

The discernment of spirits is guided by acquired and infused prudence and the gift of counsel. In the purgative stage, the spirit of the world or nature predominates. In the illuminative stage, the Spirit of God takes a hold of a person's spiritual journey. The spirit of the devil is identifiable and slowly being destroyed.

The Spirit of the Devil
The spirit of the devil is marked by pride, discouragement, despair, scrupulosity, boasting, dissension, hatreds, false humility, presumption, fear of correction, self-infatuation, bitter zeal, forgetfulness of God, lack of obedience, and an intense dislike for mortification. All that is contrary to the honor and glory of God is found in the influences of the devil.

The Spirit of the World
The spirit of the world bears a lot in common with the spirit of the devil. However, the spirit of the world does not bear the extreme evil that is indicative of the ways of the devil. In this phase, a person has very little regard for the infused virtues of faith, hope, and love. A person in this stage is

---

[199] Cf. Ignatius, *Spiritual Exercises*, 4th week.

pleasure and self-oriented. One is easily irritated and discouraged. One is indifferent to the glory and honor of God. One is indifferent to the love of God and the love of neighbor. There is no zeal in such a person. Tepidity, mediocrity, and false moderation are indicative of a person's spiritual life. People influenced by the spirit of the world (or nature) are people who are more social workers than disciples. They are the ones who at the first sign of difficulty in the spiritual life, abandon it, and go to their former way of life. They are people who are evangelized more by the world than the Gospel.

The Spirit of God

> But the fruit of the Spirit is love, joy, peace, patience, kindness, goodness, faithfulness, gentleness, self-control; against such there is no law. And those who belong to Christ Jesus have crucified the flesh with its passions and desires (Gal. 5:22-24).

All that is of the spirit of God is directed toward the honor and glory of God. Those who live in this manner bear the marks of faith, hope, and love. They are people of true, authentic humility bearing profound self-knowledge and a zeal for God. They are a people marked by interior joy and forgetfulness of self. They embrace suffering, the sweetness of the cross, and mortification. They have no regard for the world's standards of success or the world's scorn.

Authentic mortification takes place in those embraced with the Spirit of God. That which is of the Spirit of God in terms of mortification is always marked by respect for the body as the temple of God. Mortification that flows from the grace of God is moderated by discretion and obedience. A person engaged in mortification does not seek to attract attention, and he or she does not seek to damage his or her health. Rather, authentic mortification is directed toward purifying the heart and the will for the honor and glory of God.

The illuminative stage is exemplified by a person's ability to discern the spirits and to persevere in the Spirit of God. As St. John Climacus states:

> It is characteristic of the [profoundly holy] that they always know whether a thought comes from within themselves, or from God, or from the demons.... The eyes of the heart are enlightened by discernment to things seen and unseen....[200]

---

[200] *John Climacus: The Ladder of Divine Ascent*, 255.

Perceiving Christ in Others

Carryll Houselander, while traveling on a crowded underground train during rush hour in London, experienced this profound sense of seeing all people as Christs.

> I was in an underground train, a crowded train in which all sorts of people jolted together, sitting and strap-hanging—workers of every description going home at the end of the day. Quite suddenly I saw with my mind, but as vividly as a wonderful picture, Christ in them all. But I saw more than that; not only was Christ in every one of them, living in them, dying in them, rejoicing in them, sorrowing in them—but because He was in them, and because they were here, the whole world was here too, here in this underground train; not only the world as it was at that moment, not only the people in all the countries of the world, but all those people who had lived in the past, and all those yet to come. I came out into the street and walked for a long time in the crowds. It was the same here, on every side, in every passer-by, everywhere—Christ.[201]

This sense of the everywhere of Christ is expressed in a prayer ascribed to St. Patrick:

> Christ be with me, Christ within me, Christ behind me, Christ before me, Christ beside me, Christ to win me, Christ to comfort me and restore me, Christ beneath me, Christ above me, Christ in the hearts of all that love me, Christ in the mouth of friend and stranger.

Patrick sought to experience a world engulfed in Christ.

Prayer in the Illuminative Stage—Meditation to Contemplation

What began in the passive purification of the senses continues more profoundly in the illuminative stage of spirituality. Meditation is being transformed into contemplation. If one perseveres in the meditative life, meditation slowly becomes more simplified to such an extent that the various experiences and acts involved in meditation begin to fuse into a single act. The person's core being has been made docile to the workings of the Holy Spirit. The person's experience of prayer is raised to that of contemplation.

---

[201] Caryll Houselander, *A Rocking-Horse Catholic* (New York: Sheed and Ward, 1955), 137-138.

Contemplation is a mutual sharing among friends, a mutual presence, an inter-indwelling, a gaze on the guest within (Cf. 1 Jn. 4:16).[202] It is a pure supernatural gift, an inflaming of love.[203] The *Song of Songs* in the Scriptures is the perfect analogy for the experience that occurs in the silence of the soul in contemplation. One who experiences contemplation is transformed into a person of great virtue, into a person of profound works (Mt. 7:20). The following are key aspects of the fruits of contemplation:[204]

- Peace, quietude, calm, repose, serenity, and rest beyond a understanding (Cf. Phil. 4:4-7).
- A knowledge of realities that transcend the natural means of knowing
- A deepening, wounding, inflaming, engulfing, inflowing, longing love that is caused by God's self-communicating triune nature.
- Transformation into the image and likeness of God.

Contemplation is an act of the intellect that is superior to reasoning. It is simple glance at truth, which springs from love. It is an act that proceeds from faith and is enlightened by the gifts of the Holy Spirit, especially wisdom and understanding. In the beginning, contemplation can be prepared for by the reading of sacred Scripture, meditation, prayers of petitions, and centering prayer. This helps to prepare the person to experience contemplation. With time, however, these preparatory acts will not be necessary.[205] At this stage God himself will teach and refresh the core of the person without meditation or any active effort.[206] Contemplation thus becomes, in the words of St. John of the Cross, the "science of love," which is an infused knowledge of God.[207]

Degrees of Prayer in the Illuminative Stage

St. Teresa of Avila and St. John of the Cross describe most profoundly the various degrees of prayer in the illuminative way:[208]

1. The discursive meditations that survive the passive purification of the senses continue to transform the person as that person continues to grow in the virtues. As one progresses in the spiritual journey, meditation will give way to initial infused contemplation.
   a. St. John of the Cross sets a threefold guideline in determining when to progress from meditation to contemplation. First,

---

[202] *Life*, Ch. 8, no. 5 and Ch. 10, no. 1; *Way*, Ch. 27.

[203] Ibid., Ch. 23, no. 5; Ch. 24, nos. 7-8; Ch. 39, no. 23.

[204] Ibid., Ch. 27, no. 4; *Ascent*, BK II, Chs. 12-15; *Dark Night*, BK I, no. 1, and Chs. 5, 8-13, 17; *Spiritual Canticle*, St. 39, no. 12.

[205] IIa IIae, q. 180, a.3, 4, 6, 7 ad 1um; IIa IIae, q. 8, a.1, 2, 4, 6, 7; q. 45, a.1, 2, 5, 6;

[206] *Dark Night*, BK I, Ch. 14.

[207] Ibid., BK II, Ch. 18.

[208] Cf. *Life*, Chs. 11-19.

one should experience no comfort in the imagination or the senses in one's attempts at meditation. Second, the memory that lingers on in prayer is one that is filled with anxiety, with a sense that makes one feel that one is going backwards or not serving God. Finally, one is consciously aware of an inability to meditate or engage in reflections, or to excite the imagination.[209]

2. The second degree of prayer in the illuminative way can be pictured as a pump or water-wheel that draws up water. This second degree requires much less effort and yields much more water, much more spiritual fruit. This is the stage of prayer that Teresa calls the "prayer of quiet."[210] It is that level of prayer where the will is seized and held.[211] This "prayer of quiet" has three distinct phases: In the first phase, the person's will experiences a sweet and loving sense of being absorbed by God. In the second phase the person experiences a sense of quiet tranquility because the will is now not only absorbed by God but it is now captivated by God. In the third phase, the will is still captivated and the person's ability to understand what is happening to his or her soul is no longer perceivable. The virtues flower, and the soul is docile in responding to the gift of piety. Yet, in this "prayer of quiet" the person is still susceptible to distractions in prayer, for the intellect, the memory and the imagination still continue to enter into the prayer experience.[212] Centering prayer becomes very good at this stage of the spiritual journey.

3. The third degree in the prayer life in the illuminative stage can be described in a way similar to a person who irrigates his or her garden with running water. Another image used is that of water overflowing unto a riverbank and washing up onto a garden. This is the type of prayer that is often referred to as the "prayer of simple union." God's self-communicating presence at this stage is such that the interior faculties at the core of the person are now put to sleep. It is a time where the intellect is seized and held, and it is a time when the exterior senses and the imagination "fall asleep." It is often an ecstatic state.[213] God is the object of all the activities of the inner core of the person. There is no longer any wandering. A person's will,

---

[209] *Dark Night*, BK I, Ch. 9.
[210] *Life*, 14f.
[211] *Interior Castle*, 5th mansion, Ch. 1.
[212] *Life*, Chs. 14 and 17; *Interior Castle*, 4th mansion, Ch. 2.
[213] *Interior Castle*, 5th mansion, Ch. 1.

thought, imagination and memory are captivated and absorbed by God. All things are calmed. There is no more restlessness.[214]

4. There is a fourth degree of prayer in the life of a person that is called the "prayer of union." It is, however, that degree of prayer that is reserved to those who reach the highest stage of the spiritual journey, the unitive stage. It is the prayer of the mystics.[215] This is the stage in the spiritual journey that is marked by the prayer of "transforming union" or "mystical union."[216] It is like a gentle, abundant rainfall that nourishes a garden completely. The person does nothing to water the garden. It is all God's doing.[217] This reality is described by St. Bernard of Clairvaux in his *Sermon* 74:

I remember afterwards that he had been with me; sometimes I had a presentiment that he would come, but I was never conscious of his coming or his going. And where he comes from when he visits my soul, and where he goes, and by what means he enters and goes out, I admit that I do not know even now…. The coming of the Word was not perceptible to my eyes, for he has not color; nor to the ears, for there was no sound; nor yet to my nostrils, for he mingles with the mind, not the air; he has not acted upon the air, but created it. His coming was not tasted by the mouth, for there was not eating or drinking, nor could he be known by the sense of touch, for he is not tangible. How then did he enter? Perhaps he did not enter because he does not come from outside? He is not one of the things which exist outside us. Yet he does not come from within me, for he is good, and I know there is no good in me. I have ascended to the highest in me, and look! the word is towering above that. In my curiosity I have descended to explore my lowest depths, yet I found him even deeper. If I look outside myself, I saw him stretching beyond the furthest I could see; and if I looked within, he was yet further within. Then I knew the truth of what I had read, "in him we live and move and have our being." And blessed is the man in whom he has his being, who lives for him and is moved by him.[218]

---

[214] *Life*, Ch. 18f.
[215] Cf. Ibid., Ch. 18f.
[216] *Interior Castle*, 7th mansion, Ch. 3.
[217] *Life*, Ch. 11, no. 7.
[218] *Bernard of Clairvaux: On the Song of Songs IV*, trans. Kilian Walsh, O.C.S.O (Kalamazoo: Cistercian Publications, 1980), Sermon 74.

The Our Father[219]

> [This] prayer, the Our Father, contains the fullness of perfection. It was the Lord Himself who gave it to us as both an example and a rule.... It lifts them up to that prayer of fire known to so few. It lifts them up, rather, to that ineffable prayer which rises above all human consciousness with no voice sounding, no tongue moving, no words uttered. The soul lights up with heavenly illumination and no longer employs constricted, human speech.[220]

In the *Our Father* Jesus teaches us how to pray. Since he experienced all things we experience, except sin, he knows well our needs (cf. Heb. 4:15). Jesus in the *Our Father* teaches us the summary of the whole Gospel, the summary of what new life in God is all about. In this prayer one is empowered by the Spirit to cry out "abba," "Father" (cf. Jn. 6:63; Gal. 4:6)! In the Lord's Prayer one is brought into the presence of the Father, of the Trinity. In the *Our Father* one enters a prayer of "straightforward simplicity, filial trust, joyous assurance, humble boldness, and certainty of being loved"[221] (cf. Eph. 3:12; Heb. 3:6; 4:16; 10:19; 1 Jn. 2:28; 3:21; 5:14). As a prayer the *Our Father* reveals the Father and reveals one's own innermost being: It enlightens one to the Father and to one's core self.

Our Father

By saying "Our Father" one is saying that one is entering a relationship. He is our God and we are his people (cf. Jn. 1:17; Hos. 2:21-22; 6:1-6). One accepts the reality that one has also entered a relationship that implies not individualism but a sense of communion, of membership. One is a member of God's Body, the Church, the community of faith (cf. Acts 4:32; Jn. 11:52). One recognizes that the communion between the three Persons of the Trinity must be modeled by God's people, who were and are created in the image and likeness of God. Prayer is always therefore a community-oriented experience. Even in what appears to be private prayer, one is in prayer with the unknown and with the angels and saints.

---

[219] See CCC 2777-2856.
[220] *John Cassian: Conferences*, Trans. Colm Luibheid (Mahwah: Paulist Press, 1985), Conference 9, n. 25.
[221] CCC 2778

Who art in heaven

> "Our Father who art in heaven" is rightly understood to mean that God is in the hearts of the just, as in his holy temple. At the same time, it means that those who pray should desire the one they invoke to dwell in them.[222]

The phrase "who art in heaven" is not primarily a reference to a place because heaven is not a "place" as commonly understood. Heaven is a place in the sense that it is a dimension beyond space and time: Heaven is another dimension of reality. Consequently the phrase, used in the context of this prayer, is primarily a reference to God's majesty and his presence in the heart of the just. Heaven, "the Father's house, is the true homeland toward which we are heading and to which, already, we belong."[223]

Hallowed be thy name

The phrase "Hallowed be thy name" is a phrase that conjures up the holiness, preciousness, and majesty of God (cf. Ps 8:5; Isa. 6:3). It reminds one that God is worthy of all praise and thanksgiving (cf. Ps 111:9; Lk. 1:49).

Thy Kingdom Come

God's kingdom became present in the first coming and will find its fulfillment in the second coming (cf. Tit. 2:13). As a follower of Christ one is called to help bring about the fulfillment of this kingdom. A person is called upon to help build the kingdom of God here on earth, a kingdom of love.

Thy will be done on earth as it is in heaven

This phrase is an affirmation that
1) all are called to be saved and come to the truth (cf. 1 Tim. 2:3-4; 2 Pet 3:9; Mt. 18:14).
2) all must love one another (Jn. 13:34; cf. 1 Jn. 3; 4; Lk. 10: 25-37).
3) one must do all things according to God's will (Eph. 1:9-11).
4) all are called to imitate Christ in his obedience and surrendering to the Father's will (Heb. 10:7; Lk. 22:42; Jn. 4:34; 5:30; 6:38; 8:29; Gal. 1:4).

---

[222] St. Augustine, *De serm. Dom. In monte* 2, 5, 18: PL 34, 1277.
[223] CCC 2802

Give us this day our daily bread

This statement is an expression of God's goodness, a goodness that transcends all other goodness. The "Our" reminds one that one is a member of a community, a community built upon the foundation of solidarity. It is a call in trust and in a spirit of surrender to God; it is a call for God to meet the individual and the community's material and spiritual needs. It is a call to responsibility and justice (cf. Lk. 16:19-31; Mt. 25:31-46).

Another aspect of this phrase reminds the individual of the most important food of all, the Word of God and the Eucharist, the Body, Blood, Soul and Divinity of Christ. Without this food, Christian life is impossible, for it is the food of immortality. As St. Augustine and St. Peter Chrysologus point out, respectively:

> The Eucharist is our daily bread. The power belonging to this divine food makes it a bond of union. Its effect is then understood as unity, so that, gathered into his Body and made members of him, we may become what we receive.... This also is our daily bread: the readings you hear each day in church and the hymns you hear and sing. All these are necessities for our pilgrimage.[224] The Father in heaven urges us, as children of heaven, to ask for the bread of heaven. [Christ] himself is the bread who, sown in the Virgin, raised up in the flesh, kneaded in the Passion, baked in the oven of the tomb, reserved in churches, brought to altars, furnishes the faithful each day with food from heaven.[225]

And forgive us our trespasses as we forgive those who trespass against us

Love of God and love of neighbor are one reality. Any authentic love of God implies the love of neighbor, and any authentic love of neighbor implies an authentic love of God. How can a person love God if he or she does not love his or her neighbor (cf. 1 Jn. 4:20; Mt. 5: 43-44; 6:14-15; 5:23-24; 18:23-35; Mk. 11:25)? How can an individual ask for God's forgiveness if that individual is unwilling to forgive those whom God loves?

And lead us not into temptation

This petition is a call to be set free from the snares of evil. The spirit of discernment and strength become intrinsic to this petition. The Spirit guides one to determine between temptations, trials and tribulations that are for

---

[224] St. Augustine, *Sermo* 57, 7: PL 38, 389.
[225] St. Peter Chrysologus, *Sermo* 67: PL 52, 392; cf. Jn. 6:51.

one's personal growth in the life of God (cf. Lk. 8:13-15; Acts 14:22; Rm. 5:3-5; 2 Tim. 3:12) and those temptations, trials and tribulations that lead to sin and death (cf. Jas. 1:14-15). One discerns the difference between being tempted (which is not sinful and in fact can lead to great spiritual growth) and consenting to temptation. The Spirit helps discern and unmask the lies behind the temptations (cf. Gen. 3:6) and helps one to persevere through them to become strong in God (cf. 1 Cor. 10:13; Rev. 16:15).

But deliver us from evil

This is a petition that asks for protection from the cunning of the devil (cf. Jn. 17:15). The devil seeks to distort God's providential plan and seeks to destroy people in the process under the guise of doing good for them (cf. Jn. 8:44; Rev. 12:9). One finds confidence in this petition in that just as one has been delivered from evil in the past, one will be delivered from the evil one in the present and in the future if one perseveres in the spiritual battle.

> The Lord who has taken away your sin and pardoned your faults also protects you and keeps you from the wiles of your adversary the devil, so that the enemy, who is accustomed to leading into sin, may not surprise you. One who entrusts himself to God does not dread the devil. "If God is for us, who is against us?"[226]

---

[226] St. Ambrose, *De Sacr.* 5, 4, 30: PL 16, 454; cf. Rm. 8:31.

VII
The Second Dark Night
The Passive Purification of the Spirit
(or Passive Purification of the Spiritual Soul)

For a short time he allows us to taste how sweet he is, and before our taste is satisfied he withdraws; and it is in this way, by flying above us with wings outspread, that he encourages us to fly and says in effect: See now, you have had a little taste of how sweet and delightful I am, but if you wish to have your fill of this sweetness, hasten after me, drawn by my sweet-smelling perfumes, lift up your heart to where I am at the right hand of God the Father. There you will see me not darkly in a mirror but face to face, and "your heart's joy will be complete and no one shall take this joy away from you"....[227]

Guigo II

At the end of the illuminative stage of the spiritual life, one encounters the second *dark night*, the passive purification of the spirit. The passive purification of the spirit is a "mystical death" to self that takes place within the person.

During the illuminative stage God has given the person, in a sense, a rest from the pain of the first *dark night*, the purification of the senses. Now God desires to complete the purification that began in the very beginning of the spiritual journey. While a person at this level of the spiritual journey is a person who is clearly a saint, a person at this level is still in need of fine-tuning.

In the passive purification of the senses that beginners often experience, the person is purified of sensible consolations that he or she might find his or her being excessively attached to. In the passive purification of the spirit one is being divested of any remaining stains of superficial knowledge in matters pertaining to God. The remaining defects in the will and the intellect, and the remaining weaknesses of intellectual and spiritual pride still need to be conquered. In the *dark night* of the senses the main battle that took place was over temptations against chastity and patience. In the dark night of the spirit, the main battle is over the temptations against faith and hope.

---

[227] *Guigo II: The Ladder of Monks*, quoted in Egan, 211.

God at this stage is stripping the person to the core. Every aspect of the person, particularly the person's ways of thinking and praying, are being made anew. One feels at this stage deprived of God's divine illumination, his divine light. Darkness appears. One is experiencing a pain worse than martyrdom. The suffering at this stage is the ultimate purifier. As St. John of the Cross puts it:

> God divests the faculties, affections, and senses, both spiritual and sensory, interior and exterior. He leaves the intellect in darkness, the will in aridity, the memory in emptiness, and the affections in supreme affliction, bitterness, and anguish by depriving the soul of the feeling and satisfaction it previously obtained from spiritual blessings.[228]

This is a time of great sadness. "My God, my God, why have you forsaken me?" is the cry of the person in this predicament. One feels alone, abandoned, lost, no longer loved, on the verge of despair. One feels as if he or she is being ripped apart, torn down. One becomes painfully aware of one's wretchedness and one's need for God. The only thing that keeps the person going is the grace-driven hunger for God and the desire of being purified for him. The call is to walk in pure faith, in pure hope, and in pure love, which is pure darkness for the faculties of the person.[229]

Why the Suffering? Why the Darkness?

> Truly, truly, I say to you, unless a grain of wheat falls into the earth and dies, it remains alone; but if it dies, it bears much fruit. He who loves his life loses it, and he who hates his life in this world will keep it for eternal life (Jn. 12:24-25).

At this stage of the spiritual journey one enters into darkness not because of a lack of God's light, but because of an excess of God's divine light, his divine presence. The divine presence is so powerful that it transcends the capacity of the person's being to contain it. This blindness can be compared to looking into the sun directly. The sun is so bright that it blinds the sight.[230]

This divine light inevitably causes suffering, for its goal is to purify the soul of all that is not for the honor and glory of God. It is a suffering caused by the

---

228 *Dark Night*, BK II, Ch. 3,3.
229 Ibid., BK II, Chs. 4; 5; 8f.
230 Ibid., Chs. 5 and 12.

purification of any impurities still left in the core of the person's being. A purifying light, a spiritual fire is ridding the person's inner being of all its stains, of all that is contrary to love, faith and hope, of all aspects of ignorance, self-infatuation, half-truths, inordinate desires for consolations, and imperfections of any kind. It is an earthly purgatory. The cleansing words of the Scriptures come alive here: "The Lord our God is a devouring fire...(Dt. 4:24). From on high he sent fire; into my bones he made it descend...(Lam. 1:13). [Like] gold in a furnace he tried [me], and like a sacrificial burnt offering he accepted [me]" (Wis. 3:6). [231]

In this purifying fire of grace, God is healing the inner being. He is transforming the person into Christ by detaching him or her of all so that all he or she can see is God himself. The person is being prepared for intimacy with God. The person is being prepared for a "mystical death," a death to self and a new birth in the splendor of God. One is becoming nothing so that one can become everything!

What must one do to get through this stage?

One must heed the words of St. John of the Cross: "God teaches the soul secretly and instructs it in the perfection of love without its doing anything or understanding how this happens."[232]   Because of this reality one must be completely abandoned to the divine will and to divine providence (Rom. 4:18).[233] One must pray for perseverance, and live by faith, hope and love. One must carry one's cross and unite oneself with Christ's passion (Cf. Rom. 1:17). One must abandon oneself to God's mercy and pray for the intercession of the saints, and particularly the intercession of the Blessed Mother. One must cry out in the words of the Psalmist, "Thou art holy, enthroned on the praises of Israel. In thee our fathers trusted; they trusted and thou didst deliver them" (Ps. 22:3-4).

The Precious Outcome of the Burning Flame

The theological virtues of faith, hope, and love, with the help of the Spirit's gifts of understanding, knowledge, and piety are elevated to heights previously unknown. Because of this reality, one becomes a new creation in Christ. There are no longer any vestiges of spiritual and intellectual pride, no vestiges of selfish attraction to one's own way of seeing, feeling, and willing, and no vestiges of rudeness, impatience, bitter zeal, jealousy, slander, discord, delusions, or unconscious egoism.

---

[231] Ibid., Chs.5, 10, and 12; *Treatise*, BK II, Ch. 1.
[232] *Dark Night*, BK II, Ch. 5, 1.
[233] Treatise, BK IX, Chs. 3-6; 12-16.

One who comes out of the *dark night of the spirit* has entered the unitive stage of spirituality. The person has become an open treasure chest to God's love. One is living in a new realm. One seeks to be nothing, so that God may be everything, and by so seeking nothing one becomes everything. One seeks to love God for simply being God, as opposed to loving God for what he can give. Love truly becomes as strong as death for such a person (Song of Songs 8:6). One begins to see the world the way Christ sees the world; that is, to see the world the way the world truly is. Guided by the gifts of knowledge and understanding, one delves into the mysteries of God that transcend the limits of human reason.[234]

After a long journey in this *dark night* one can say with St. Therese of Lisieux:

> [In] the crucible of trials from within and without, my soul has been refined, and I can raise my head like a flower after a storm and see how the words of the Psalm have been fulfilled in my case: "The Lord is my Shepherd and I shall want nothing."[235]

---

[234] Cf. *Dark Night*, BK II, Chs. 2, 5, 9; IIa IIae, q. 8, a.1, 8.
[235] St. Therese, *Story of a Soul*, 3.

VIII
The Unitive Stage
A Taste of Heaven

There is no other path than through the burning love of the crucified.... For no one is in any way disposed for divine contemplation that leads to mystical ecstasy unless like Daniel he is a man of desires (Dan. 9:23).[236]

St. Bonaventure

The unitive stage of spirituality is the realm where the mystics live. This is the stage where a new transformation has taken place within the very core of the person. A new life begins here, a life like nothing ever before, a life that will only be surpassed in its bliss by the experience of heaven itself.

It is a stage where one has entered the ultimate sphere of being dissolved in God.[237] It is a realm where the Spirit's gifts of wisdom, understanding, counsel, fortitude, knowledge, piety, wonder and awe come to their fullest expression. It is where the fruits of the Spirit such as charity, joy, peace, patience, benignity, goodness, mildness, faith, modesty, and chastity are enjoyed. It is where the capital sins of pride, covetousness, lust, anger, gluttony, envy, sloth are non-existent.

The unitive stage is the stage of heroes. It is the stage where heroic virtue is lived out in its ultimate expression.[238]

The Heroic Theological Virtues
Faith

I am never afraid. I am doing my work with Jesus, I'm doing it for Jesus, I'm doing it to Jesus, and therefore the results are His, not mine. If you need a guide, you only have to look to Jesus. You have to surrender to Him and rely on Him completely. When you do this, all doubt is dispelled and you are filled with conviction.[239]

Mother Teresa

---

[236] Bonaventure, *The Soul's Journey into God*, trans. Evert Cousins (Mahwah: Paulist Press, 1979), n. 5.

[237] Cf. IIa IIae, q. 24, a.9.

[238] Cf. Ia IIae, q. 61, a.5, q.69.

[239] *Mother Teresa: A Simple Path*, compiled by Lucinda Vardey (New York: Ballantine Books, 1995), 44.

Faith at this stage in the spiritual journey is exemplified by its penetration, firmness, and promptness. A person of such profound faith is a person capable of penetrating the deepest mysteries of divine revelation. Such a person lives life contemplating all things in light of God's will. Reality is seen the way it really, authentically is: It is seen the way God sees it. Because of this deep penetration and firmness of faith, a person at this level of faith adheres not only to the great mysteries of the faith, but also to the most obscure aspects. There are no "cafeteria" Catholics at this stage of the faith. Promptness in decisions regarding one's eternal destiny and the eternal destiny of others becomes paramount. The great insight acquired at this level of life makes the rejection of errors easy, for all that is not of God screams emptiness. A person in the unitive stage of spirituality can be said to have a contemplative faith.[240]

Hope

There is a complete surrendering to God's will and his providence at this level of hope. Aided by the Spirit's gift of wisdom a person can live out the heroic life of hope in such a way that all the trials and tribulations of life are responded to with the words, "I can do all things in him who strengthens me" (Phil. 4:13). One firmly chants: "If God is for us, who [can be] against us" (Rom. 8:31)? Trust in God at this plateau is unequalled. The words of Luke 11:9-10 become reality: "Ask, and it will be given you; seek, and you will find; knock, and it will be opened to you. For every one who asks receives, and he who seeks finds, and to him who knocks it will be opened."

At this plateau in the spiritual life, hope becomes transformed into a sense of invisible trust, abandonment, and firmness in one's eternal destiny, life with God in heaven. While heaven is never assured on this earthly journey, for God's love always requires a response, the sense of one's eternal destiny attains a firmness that makes turning away from God almost impossible. In a sense, a person feels that he or she has reached the *point of no return*. One feels that to turn back would be a loss of such catastrophic proportions that one would cease to exist.

Love

Love of God and love of neighbor become experienced beyond anything that has ever been experienced before. One loves God completely for just being God. No more is there a longing for what I can get from God or what I can get from my neighbor by loving him or her. One loves God completely for just being God. One loves one's neighbor for simply being the image of God

---

[240] Cf. IIa IIae, q.8, a.1,3.

As Evargrius Ponticus, the desert Father mentions, "Happy is the...[person] who considers all [people] as god—after God."[241]

At this stage the love of God and the love of neighbor become for all practical purposes a single reality. To authentically love God one needs to authentically love one's neighbor and to authentically love one's neighbor one has to authentically love God.

The person at this stage of love grasps the mystery of the intimacy of Christ's human will with his divine will. The human will of Jesus was in complete conformity with his divine will. One who experiences the heights of heroic love experiences a taste of this mystery of wills. While it is true that a person does not have two wills, nor two natures like the God-man Jesus Christ, a person's single, human will and God's will can become, because of love, one. While God's nature and the nature of the human spiritual person are distinct realities, that human spiritual person can grow in response to God's grace to such a level of love that that person's every desire and action can become in conformity with God's. Two truly become spiritually one. One truly becomes, as the Fathers of the Church so often echoed, *divinized*.

Consequently, love of the cross reaches its apex in the unitive stage of love, for within the cross is the mystery of Christ's love.

> Let's fix our eyes on the cross. What do we see? We see his head bent down to kiss us. Look at his hands. They say, "I love you!" We see his arms stretched out on the cross as if to embrace us. We see his heart opened wide to receive us. That is the cross, which is represented by the crucifix that most of us have in our homes. Each time we glance at it, it should help us to fall in love with Christ. It should help us to love him with sincerity of heart. What greater love is there than God's love for each of us? ....[242]

> Suffering—pain, humiliation, sickness and failure is but a kiss of Jesus. Suffering is a gift of God, a gift that makes us most Christ-like. People must not accept suffering as a punishment.... Any who imitate Jesus to the full must also share in his passion. Suffering is meant to purify, to sanctify, to make us Christ-like.[243]
>
> *Mother Teresa*

---

[241] Evargrius Ponticus, *The 153 Chapters on Prayer*, 123, in Harvey Egan, *An Anthology of Mysticism (Collegeville*, The Liturgical Press, 1991), 52.

[242] Mother Teresa, *One Heart Full of Love*, 95.

[243] Mother Teresa, *Words to Love By...* (New York: Walker and Company, 1983), 61-67.

The Heroic Moral Virtues
Humility

In the unitive stage humility is experienced as never before. Humility is essentially self-knowledge. To know oneself the way one truly is is what humility is all about. The person is now seeing himself or herself the way God sees him or her. Self-knowledge at this stage is now uncluttered by inordinate self-infatuation. It is uncluttered from all things that hinder self-knowledge and the powerful imitation of Christ and the majesty of God reflected in all creatures.[244]

Humility finds its greatest expression at this stage in a person's ability to take ridicule, abasement, and humiliation without any concern for one's own self. Such persons see these assaults as opportunities to share in the cross of Jesus Christ.

This stage is a period of extraordinary modesty. There is no conceit or vanity in such a person.

Meekness

"Blessed are the meek, for they shall inherit the earth" (Mt. 5:5). One who is meek is patient and gentle. This is the stage of a person's walk in grace that leads to perfect self-mastery—as perfect as is possible on this earthly journey. One does not return evil with evil. One dominates one's passions, particularly the passion of unjustified anger. A person finds no disturbance in being injured; rather, one experiences great empathy and compassion for the one doing the injuring.[245] St. Francis of Assisi exemplified the reality of this heroic virtue in his legendary prayer of gentleness:

> Lord, make me an instrument of your peace.
> Where there is hatred, let me sow love.
> Where there is injury, pardon.
> Where there is doubt, faith.
> Where there is despair, hope.
> Where there is darkness, light.
> Where there is sadness, joy.
> O Divine Master,
> grant that I may not so much seek
> to be consoled as to console;
> to be understood as to understand;

---

[244] Cf. IIa IIae, q. 160, a.1, 2; q. 161, a.1, 3, 6 ad 3um.
[245] Cf. IIa IIae, q. 157, a.1, 2, 4.

to be loved as to love.
For it is in giving that we receive;
it is in pardoning that we are pardoned;
and it is in dying that we are born to eternal life.

Fortitude

There are always souls to enlighten, sinners to pardon, tears to dry, disappointments to console, sick to encourage, children and youngsters to guide. There is, there ever shall be, [people] to love and save, in Christ's name! This is your vocation; it ought to make you happy and courageous.[246]

Pope John Paul II

Here the moral virtue of fortitude or courage is magnified by the Spirit's gift of fortitude. A person at this stage of his or her life is able to pursue in an extraordinary way that which is very difficult to do but which is very necessary to do. Fear, danger, fatigue, criticism, and so forth, are dominated and mastered. All that one undertakes is taken with great courage, from the simplest task to the most difficult.

Magnanimity

Closely associated with the gift of fortitude is the gift of magnanimity— the ability to endure trials for extended periods of time with patience and courage. Martyrdom is the quintessential expression of this grace-elevated virtue.[247] In the spiritual diaries of St. John de Brebeuf one reads the following account of the spirit of this virtue:

For two days now I have experienced a great desire to be a martyr and to endure all the torments the martyrs suffered.

Jesus, my Lord and Savior, what can I give you in return for all the favors you have first conferred on me? I will take from your hand the cup of your sufferings and call on your name. I vow before your eternal Father and the Holy Spirit, before your most holy Mother and her most chaste spouse, before the angels, apostles and martyrs, before my blessed fathers Saint Ignatius and Saint Francis Xavier—in truth I vow to you, Jesus my Savior, that as far as I have

---

[246] John Paul II, *Prayers and Devotions* (New York: Viking, 1994), 299.
[247] Cf. IIa IIae, q. 123, a.6.

the strength I will never fail to accept the grace of martyrdom, if some day you in your infinite mercy should offer it to me, your most unworthy servant.

I bind myself in this way so that for the rest of my life I will have neither permission nor freedom to refuse opportunities of dying and shedding my blood for you, unless at a particular juncture I should consider it more suitable for your glory to act otherwise at that time. Further, I bind myself to this so that, on receiving the blow of death, I shall accept it from your hands with the fullest delight and joy of spirit. For this reason, my beloved Jesus, and because of the surging joy which moves me, here and now I offer my blood and body and life. May I die only for you, if you will grant me this grace, since you willingly died for me. Let me so live that you may grant me the gift of such a happy death. In this way, my God and Savior, I will take from your hand the cup of your sufferings and call on your name: Jesus, Jesus, Jesus![248]

Prudence

Prudence at this level is exemplified by the perfect acting out of that which is best for one or another's eternal destiny. It is the unique moral virtue that enables a person to determine a reasonable milieu between excess and deficiency. Inconsideration, indecision, inconstancy, or rashness is non-existent at this point. A person at this point recognizes the true good and is able to direct the other virtues to accomplish this good. Prudence at this stage is powerfully engulfed by the Spirit's gift of counsel to such an extent that one inevitably experiences a supernatural sense or intuition of what ought to be done or not done. The hunger for truth is the focus of this stage in the experience of the virtue of prudence.[249]

Justice

Immense distress moves us to launch a cry of alarm. Where is love for those who have been refused the right to live? For those who have been killed, mutilated, or imprisoned because they roam the streets? For those who have been exploited at an early age in forced labor or the commerce of perversion? For those whom famine has thrown on the roads of exile? For those who have been made to

---

[248] *The Jesuit Relations and Allied Documents* (Cleveland: The Burrow Brothers, 1898), 164, 166.
[249] Cf. IIa IIae, q. 47, a.7.

carry arms? Where is love for those who have been left without a school education and have been condemned to illiteracy?   Where is love for those whose family has been destroyed and displaced?[250]

Pope John Paul II

Justice is the upholding of what is right and fair. In the unitive stage justice takes on the heroic aspect of radically rendering to each person that which he or she is due as a child of God. Theft, fraud, lying, hypocrisy, calumny, slander, derision, simulation, raillery, and so forth, are non-existent in the person. One at this stage avoids any aspect of injustice with miraculous fervor.

This fervor, however, is accompanied by the perfect living out of *epikeia*, the spirit of the law. The person who lives the life of heroic justice is a person who, as Evargrius Ponticus describes, "considers himself one with all men because he seems constantly to see himself in every man."[251]

The Heroic Evangelical Councils
Poverty

It would be a shame for us to be richer than Jesus, who for our sake endured poverty.[252]

Mother Teresa

"Blessed are you poor, for yours is the kingdom of God" (Lk. 5:20). The focus of the mystic at this stage is on living on the bare minimum. Imitation of Christ's poverty is the desire of such a person. The mystic experiences a holy fear for those whose souls are at risk because of comfort and wealth. The contrast between the wealthy and the dying poor becomes a source of pain in the mystic. It becomes a sharing in the cross of Jesus Christ.

Chastity

Chastity becomes the great liberating gift of God at this juncture. No longer are the distractions of the flesh a hindrance to the spiritual life. In the married person, chastity enables a person to give his or her being fully, without doubt or reservation, to his or her spouse. Authentic conjugal love at its ecstatic apex takes place at this level of the relationship. For the celibate,

---

[250] John Paul II, *Papal Wisdom* (New York: Dutton, 1995), 62.
[251] Evargrius Ponticus, *The 153 Chapters on Prayer*, 125.
[252] Mother Teresa, *Heart of Joy*, 137.

freedom becomes the all-encompassing reality of existence. One is free to be fully, without doubt or reservation, a person that is radically for others.

Obedience

Self-centeredness is replaced by other-centeredness. The concern is with doing all that is for the glory and honor of God. There is an abnegation of self-will at this level. This is easily seen in the life of a holy religious. The brother or sister in a religious congregation is obedient to all orders, even the most difficult orders, even the most misguided orders, as long as they do not contradict God's will, honor, and glory. Obedience at this stage is the radical following of Christ's Way. It images the Son's obedience to his Father.

Degrees of the Unitive Life

> The lover asked his Beloved if there was anything remaining in him which was still to be loved. And the Beloved answered that he still had to love that by which his own love could be increased.[253]
>
> *Ramon Lull*

In the *passive purification of the spirit* a person encounters the experience of *arid mystical union*.[254] In the unitive stage, the person, the mystic, progresses to experience an *ecstatic union* with God and for the very few a *transforming union* in God. For the great mystics, the *transforming union*, the highest form of union with God on earth, is attained. These are the *divinized*.

Ecstatic Union

> I am wounded by love. Love urges me to speak of love. Gladly do I give myself up to the service of love…. Do you not feel as if sometimes you were shot through the heart when the fiery dart of this love penetrates the inmost mind of man, pierces his affections so that he can in no way contain or hide the burning of his desire. He burns with desire, his affections are stirred, he is in fever and gasps, sighing deeply and drawing long breaths…. Thus, the fever of love, often waning but always returning more acutely, gradually weakens the spirit, wears down and exhausts the strength, until it completely conquers the soul and lays it low.[255]

---

[253] Ramon Lull, *The Book of the Lover and Beloved*, trans. E. Allison Peers (Mahwah: Paulist Press, 1978), n. 1.

[254] *Interior Castle*, 4th and 5th mansions and chapter 1 of the 6th mansion.

Ecstasy is the suspension of the exterior senses, the loss of the use of the senses. It is a movement of the entire person's being, body and soul, toward God. It is an experience that may last a few moments, a few minutes, or at times for an entire day or days.[256] A vision at times is the prelude to this experience. But at all times, the person experiencing this ecstasy swoons as he or she becomes ravished and absorbed in the purity of God's love. The body is wounded with the wound of love. Ecstasy ends with an awakening whereby the person slowly recovers the use of the senses.[257]

Rapture

The spiritual experience of rapture is one that is experienced by some, yet it need not be experienced by all who progress toward the *transforming union*.[258] The person who experiences a rapture is a person who senses his or her very core being seized by God and carried away into another dimension of reality, a new divine region.[259] This rapture adds something to ecstasy; it adds a certain impulsive, intense, turbulent, jarring, jolting, fervent aspect to the experience.[260] It is as if the person's core is inebriated with the overabundance of God. The person's being is overwhelmed by a rushing flood of God's presence. It is not unusual to see the process toward the *spiritual marriage*--which we will take up in the next section--end in rapture.[261]

The Effects of the Ecstatic Union

The primary effect of the *ecstatic union* is the purification of love. By purifying the person's love, the person is prepared to enter in response to grace into the *transforming union*. The mystic at this level has reached the pinnacle of detachment, the pinnacle of sorrow for sin. The person has reached the apex of avoiding all that separates him or her from God. Crosses are no longer feared but embraced as a sharing in the life of the Savior. Suffering becomes a precious gift.[262]

---

[255] *Richard of Saint Victor: Selected Writings on Contemplation*, trans. Clare Kirchberger (New York: Harper and Brothers, 1957), 213-233.
[256] *Interior Castle*, 6th mansion, Ch. 6.
[257] Ibid., Ch. 2; Life, Ch. 20, par. 2; Treatise, Bk. VII, Ch. 4f.
[258] Ibid., Ch. 9.
[259] Ibid., Ch. 5.
[260] IIa IIae, q. 175, a.2 ad ium.
[261] *Interior Castle*, 6th mansion, Ch. 4.
[262] *Life*, Ch. 29; *Dark Night*, BK II, Ch. 11f; *Living Flame*, St. 1, v. 2-4; St. 2, v. 1-3.

> Resemblance to God is the whole of man's perfection. To refuse to be perfect is to be at fault.[263]
>
> *William of St. Thierry*

Once the person has progressed past the *ecstatic union*, the person reaches the summit of the mystical life, the *transforming union*. At this juncture of the mystical life one experiences the ultimate luminous, sweet, and penetrating experience of grace, of God. It is the culmination of the development of the life of grace.[264]

The essential nature of the *transforming union* is marked, as a rule, by the cessation of ecstasies. The person's very being has developed beyond this point in the spiritual journey. One's entire faculties are drawn to the very core of one's being, where the Trinity dwells.[265]

Spiritual Betrothal and Spiritual Marriage

The summit of union on this earthly journey ends in the *spiritual marriage* between a person and his or her Creator. As with every relationship that ends in marriage, there is a time of *betrothal*, a transitory time of union that awaits the *spiritual marriage*, that perfect, continuous union of life and love.[266] In the *spiritual marriage* one becomes so intimately united with God that one becomes, as St. John of the Cross so powerfully explains, God by participation:

> The spiritual marriage is incomparably greater than the spiritual betrothal, for it is a total transformation in the Beloved, in which each surrenders the entire possession of self to the other with a certain consummation of the union of love. The soul thereby becomes divine, God through participation, insofar as is possible in this life.... It is accordingly the highest state attainable in this life.[267]

Effects of the Transforming Union

The virtues and the Spirit's gifts have received their full development, a full as is humanly possible on this earthly journey. Sin for all practical purpose is no longer possible, not even venial sins. One has become in a sense deified

---

[263] *William St. Thierry: The Golden Epistle*, n. 259.
[264] *Living Flame*, St. 2; *Spiritual Canticle*, Part III, St. 22f.
[265] *Living Flame*, St. 2.
[266] *Spiritual Canticle*, St. 14-15; *Interior Castle*, 7th mansion, Ch. 2.
[267] Ibid.,St. 22,3.

One has become God by participation. For William of St. Thierry, "man becomes through grace what God is by nature."[268] And as St. John of the Cross so eloquently puts it:

[When one has reached the top of the mountain] the soul will be clothed in a new understanding of God in God (through removal of the old understanding) and in a new love of God in God, once the will is stripped of all the old cravings and satisfactions. And God will vest the soul with new knowledge when the other old ideas and images are cast aside (Col. 3:9). He causes all that is of the old self, the abilities of one's natural being, to cease, and he attires all the faculties with new supernatural abilities. As a result, one's activities, once human, now become divine.[269]

The Spiritual Senses

God be in my head and in my understanding. God be in my eyes and in my looking. God be in my mouth and in my speaking. God be in my heart and in my thinking. God be at my end and my departing.

Sarum Primer

One who has reached the level of the unitive stage experiences reality in a completely different light. One experiences what has often been referred to as the spiritualization of the senses or what is referred to as the *mystical senses*, whereby all of reality is seen differently. "It is no longer I who live" (Gal. 2:20). The person is in the sphere of spiritual sensitivity and discernment. A person enters a sphere where he or she has, in a manner, as St. Gregory of Nyssa mentions, "two sets of senses, one corporeal and the other spiritual..."[270] As Origen, one of the great ecclesiastical writers of the second century states:

Since Christ is a "fountain" and rivers of living water flow from him" (cf. Jn. 7:38), and since he is "bread" and gives "life," it should not seem strange that he is also "nard" and "gives forth fragrance" and is the "ointment" (cf. Cant. 1:12) by which those who are anointed themselves become Christ, as it says in the Psalm: "Touch not my Christs" (Ps. 105:15). And perhaps, according to what the Apostle

---

[268] *William of St. Thierry: The Golden Epistle*, n. 263.
[269] Ascent, BK 1, Ch. 5, 7.
[270] From *Glory to Glory: Texts from Gregory of Nyssa's Mystical Writings*, ed. and intro. Jean Danielou, S.J., trans. and ed. Herbert Musurillo, S.J. (New York: Charles Scribner's Son's, 1961), 156.

says, in those "who have their faculties trained by practice to distinguish good from evil (cf. Heb. 5:14), each one of the senses of the soul becomes Christ. For that is why he is called the "true light" (cf. 1 Jn. 2:8) so that the souls might have eyes with which to be illumined; and why he is called the "Word" (cf. Jn. 1:1), that they might have ears with which to hear; and why he is called "bread of life" (cf. Jn. 6:35), that the souls might have a sense of taste with which to taste. So too is he called "ointment" or "nard" so that the soul's sense of smell might receive the fragrance of the Word. And so too is he called perceivable, and touchable by hand, and the "Word became flesh" (cf. Jn. 1:14), so that the inner hand of the soul might be able to make contact with the Word of Life.... What do you think they will do when the Word of God takes over their hearing and sight and touch and taste? and when he gives to each of their senses the powers of which they are naturally capable? So that the eye, once able to see "his glory, glory as of the only Son from the Father" (Jn.1:14), no longer wants to see anything else, nor the hearing want to hear anything other than the "Word of life" (1 Jn. 1:1)..., nor will the taste, once it has "tasted the goodness of the Word of God" (Heb. 6:5) and his flesh...(Jn. 6:33, 52-58), be willing to taste anything else after this.... For just as in the body there are different senses of tasting and seeing, so are there...divine faculties of perception.[271]

Through the spiritual senses one sees reality through the eyes of God.

In Conclusion

The Christian of the future will either be a mystic or nothing at all. These are the words of the great twentieth century theologian and Jesuit priest Karl Rahner.[272] We are all called to be mystics. To the extent that one responds to God's grace is the extent that one will enter into the realm where a taste of heaven can be acquired even here on earth, where a taste of perfect happiness, peace and contentment can be found. May we all seek to become saints. May we live the words expressed by the prayer of Karl Rahner:

---

[271] From *Origen, Spirit and Fire: A Thematic Study of His Writings*, by Hans Urs von Balthasar, trans. Robert J. Daly, S.J. (Washington, D.C.: The Catholic University of America Press, 1984), 220-221.
[272] Rahner, *Theological Investigations*, vol. 7, *Further Theology of the Spiritual Life*, trans. David Bourke (New York: Herder and Herder, 1971), 15.

Son of the Father, Christ who lives in us, you are our hope of glory. Live in us, bring our life under the laws of your life, make our life like to yours. Live in me, pray in me, suffer in me, more I do not ask. For if I have you I am rich; those who find you have found the power and the victory of their life. Amen.[273]

---

[273] Rahner, *Everyday Faith*, 210-211.

Made in the USA
Charleston, SC
22 February 2017